GRO

YOUR COFFEE SHOP

(Hotel, Pub or Restaurant)

FAST

How to Dominate the

High Street And

Brew up Insane Profits

Chris Hamlett

Grow Your Coffee Shop Fast

www.growyourcoffeeshopfast.co.uk

First paperback edition published in 2017 by The Flying Coffee Company. A catalogue record for this book is available from the British Library.

ISBN 978-1-9997357-0-8

Printed in Great Britain by Catford Print Centre

Testimonials

"Grow Your Coffee Shop Fast is an interesting read that moves at pace, gives lots of sensible ideas and easy to implement advice, mixed with fun and wit. It's an easy read with serious profits for those who take the time to implement the points Chris suggests.

It will, without doubt, help small business owners think differently about their business and clearly highlights the areas they can work on their business with guaranteed results.

Implementing only half of the ideas Chris introduces in his book will help many small business owners succeed in their quest to grow their businesses"

Steve Penk - Commercial Director, La Spaziale UK Ltd

"I've known Chris for some time and know that he is a genius when it comes to providing coffee and coffee equipment, but as this book clearly demonstrates he's also got an extraordinarily good understanding of marketing. I know I'm not Chris's "target market" but I do get monthly deliveries to supply our office (and its ace coffee).

But this isn't about the coffee that Chris supplies, this is about this book.

If you run a coffee shop, are starting a coffee shop or even thinking about starting a coffee shop, this is an absolute must read. This book covers pretty much everything you need to know about marketing your coffee shop, but better than that, it gives you all the technical details you could possibly need to plan the ins and outs of actually growing your coffee shop/business.

If you dream of getting more customers for your coffee shop, or you plan on starting one soon, then I urge you – read this book and take action on all the points mentioned in it.

It's fantastic."

Ben Waters - Digital Magnet

"I loved this book. Chris has shown how you can easily develop the strategies to grow your catering business.
It's packed full of useful information which he's managed to present in a logical, clear and simple way.
This is a must read for any business but an essential read if you're just starting out.
You'll get a great deal from it."

Kay Musgrove – The George Hotel of Stamford

"Chris has written a very interesting book. I enjoyed reading it and found it to be packed full of relevant information on sales and marketing. I've been in sales for many years, even so, I've gleaned a lot of new ideas just from reading this book.

The coffee section is very good, with plenty of advice for those looking for the right coffee for their coffee shop.

Like the little anecdotes!"

Steve Goode – Wholesale Manager, Masteroast

"Love this book. Particularly because it's written on a personal level. Chris talks to the reader as an individual and shares his expertise and experiences with you. It contains a host of very informative marketing material and explains why marketing must be a planned activity. Each chapter takes you through different aspects of how to grow your business in a logical and ordered way, with great little summaries to round them off. Follow Chris's methods and you are bound to succeed in growing your business.

Then there's the details on coffee machines and coffee, which was particularly interesting to me. Great detail if you are starting a coffee shop.

To summarise, this book is a must read for anyone running a coffee shop or a coffee related business.

Good work Chris."

Richard Cook – Commercial Director, Masteroast

CONTENTS

Introduction **1**
   Your Equipment & Ingredients 2
   Marketing 3
   Who am I? 4

PART 1 .... **7**

Grow Your Coffee Business Fast **8**
   What's the Key to it All? 8
   HOLD UP! **9**

Chapter 1 .... **10**
   How to Grow your Coffee Business Fast 10
   SUMMARY 15

PART 2 .... **16**

Business Principles **17**
   The bits you ought to know before going into business.
   17

Chapter 2 .... **18**
   Most Business Owners Haven't Got a Clue 18
   Your Aims and Aspirations 19
   Branding 21
   USP 22
   Work ON your business, not IN your business 25
   SUMMARY 27

Chapter 3 .... **28**
   Business Principals 28
   The 80/20 principal 29

Customer Value 32
Cost of Marketing 33
Testing and ROI 35
Trial and Error 36
The Majority Are Wrong 37
Growing your Business 38
SUMMARY 40

PART 3 ....**41**

MARKETING **42**

Chapter 4 ....**43**
Marketing is Simple 43
Marketing is the life blood of your business 44
Marketing Plan **45**
Strategies and Tactics 46
SUMMARY 48

Chapter 5 ....**49**
Grow your coffee shop Method 1 ....**49**
Getting More Customers **49**
The Three M's **50**
1 - Your Market **51**
Who is Your Ideal Customer? 51
Who won't be your customer? 53
What are you marketing? 54
SUMMARY 56
2 – The Medium **57**
Offline **58**
Pre-Opening Marketing 58
The outside of your premises 60
Press Release 60
Advertising 61
Give Aways 61
Leaflet Drops 62

After You're Open.. 63
    Contact details... 63
    Survey Cards 65
    Loyalty Cards 65
    Referrals 66
    Newsletter 66
    Menus 67
    Book 68
    Swing Sign 69
Online 71
    Website 71
    SEO 77
    Social Media 78
Email Marketing.. 79
    Other 87
    Staff... 87
    Processes 88
    SUMMARY 90
3 - The Message.. 91
    When do you sell to them?........................ 91
    How do you sell to them? 92
    The AIDA Principal 94
    SUMMARY 99

Chapter 6 100
Grow your coffee shop Method 2 100
Sell more to your customers 100
    Selling more per visit 101
    Staff training 101
    Upselling.. 102
    Bundle stuff... 103
    New Items 103
    Retail shelf 104
    High Priced Items..................................... 104

Layout of your Coffee Shop 105
Get your Customers to visit more often **106**
Limited Offer 106
Continuity System 107
SUMMARY 108

Chapter 7 .... **109**
Grow your coffee Shop Method 3 .... **109**
Charge your customers more. **109**
Premium Positioning 109
Expert status 110
The One Thing 110
Polarisation 112
Premium Pricing **113**
Increase your prices 113
Do People Buy on Price? 113
Price Elasticity 114
Offers and Discounts 115
Quality, Service, Price 116
Pricing and Profit 117
Pricing Reviews **117**
SUMMARY 119

Chapter 8 .... **120**
Putting it all together **120**
JFDI 121
Time Management 121
Pomodoro 122
Writing 123
The Vital Factors 124
Quality Equipment & Ingredients 125
HOLD UP! 126
SUMMARY 127

PART 4 .... **128**

Chapter 9 129
Coffee & Coffee Equipment 129
Tools of the Trade.. 130
Espresso Coffee Systems 131
    What are the differences in the machines?............. 131
    Manual 132
    Semi-automatic 133
    Automatic.. 134
    Size of Machine 136
Other Variations... 138
    Steam / Water Valves... 138
    Electronic or Pressure Switch Heat Control........... 138
    Standard or Take Away Machines 139
    Integrated grinder.. 139
    Full Electronic Control... 140
    Auto-Milk Foaming 140
    Types of Coffee... 140
Espresso Grinders 141
    Grind & Dispense.. 143
    Manual 144
    Timed 144
    Automatic.. 145
    Other factors... 145
    Grind On Demand 146
    Tamping 147
    Integral with a grinder... 148
    Hand Tamper 148
    Click Tamper 149
    Automatic.. 149
Accessories 150
    Calcium Treatment Unit.. 151
    Secondary filter... 151
    Knockout Box 151
    Foaming Jugs 152

Cups 152
Thermometer and Spatula 153
Cloth 153
Other Coffee Brewing Methods 154
Bean to Cup Machine 154
Pod Systems 155
Capsule Machines 156
Filter Coffee Machines 157
Pour & Serve machines 157
Bulk Brew Coffee machines 158
Cafetiere 159
Equipment Suppliers 159
SUMMARY 162

Chapter 8 163
Coffee 163
Coffee Varieties 164
Coffee Processing 165
Coffees for Espresso 166
Coffee Beans 167
Pre-ground Coffee 167
Coffee Pods & Capsules 168
Coffees for Filter and Cafetiere 169
Artisan Coffee Roasters 169
Quality of Coffee 170
The Best Coffee 172
Certified coffees 172
Coffee Suppliers 172
SUMMARY 174

Chapter 9 175
Costs 175
Coffee 176
Equipment 176
Buying Out Right 177

Leasing 179
Continuity System 180
SUMMARY 181

Remember: - 182
And Finally: - 184

Introduction

I have written this book to give you advice on growing your coffee business, particularly if you are planning a new venture, but the concepts are equally valid for existing businesses. There are many books and websites offering guidance on the practicalities of starting a business; where to locate it, how to write a business plan, etc. There are also some specifically about setting up a coffee shop, with advice on staff requirements, funding and the like. **This book, however, is about growing your business,** and looks at the **overall concepts** of business that you need to be aware of and the **strategies** you can employ to grow it.

Much of it is also applicable to a hotel, restaurant or bar, particularly for the areas that involve coffee. It will also help you if you are planning to add to or improve your existing coffee operation.

Your Equipment & Ingredients

If it's a coffee shop you're planning, then your coffee machine is going to be the main tool of your trade. It needs to work day in, day out, be reliable and produce a consistent, quality product.

I'm always amazed when I get requests for a second-hand machine for a new coffee outlet. This is usually because too much money has been spent on refurbishments, furniture, etc. and there's not enough left for the coffee machine. Either that or the owner doesn't realise the benefits of having good quality tools and products to work with.

At the end of the day it's **your equipment** and **the ingredients** you're using that are going to provide the **products you'll be selling.** These products are a major part of **making your business a success.**

It's no good having a wonderful looking establishment and then trying to operate with inferior equipment and mediocre products. The décor may well attract the customers in the first place but to **keep them coming back will require good, quality, consistent products**, coffee being one of the main ones. The taste of the coffee will often be the taste the customer leaves with. A quality coffee, well made, will leave a pleasant after-taste and keep your customer happy. There's no excuse for using sub-standard products.

As I said, the coffee machine is the main tool of your trade. It needs to be robust and reliable. Cheap equipment or second-hand equipment is often just the opposite. A coffee shop is not a coffee shop if your coffee machine is not working.

Marketing

Although this book will cover the machines and products for the coffee section of your business the first thing you need is a marketing plan. When you started, or if you are about to start, a business you'll have prepared a business and financial plan, what you now need is a marketing plan. To start with, there has to be a focus on what you want to achieve; what do you want the feel of the coffee shop or coffee area to be like, what sort of theme are you going to adopt or have adopted, what type of customer do you want to attract.

The first part of this book will look at business in general and discuss the topics you may not have even considered. They are, however, vital to the success of every business, including yours.

Then we'll get down to the strategies and tactics you can use in your marketing.

The last part will look at the coffee section of your business, the machines, the coffee, and associated activities and how these relate to the topics discussed in the first section

Who am I?

I am Chris, the owner of The Flying Coffee Company. I supply coffee outlets with coffee machines, coffees and a host of related products. I have a great team who run the day to day business, and together we run training sessions on espresso coffees and barista skills, and cover machine servicing as well. Let me be clear here, I have never run a coffee shop, but I've been in the coffee supply business in various guises for twenty odd years or so. During this time, I've supplied many varied businesses, hotels, restaurants, offices, but mainly coffee shops. I've seen and worked with many start-ups as well as established businesses. Some have flourished, some have ticked along nicely, and some have failed. The same is true for my suppliers and I now work with the reliable ones that provide me with a good service, good products and excellent backup. They are not necessarily the cheapest, but at the end of the day you get what you pay for. Reliable suppliers have been an essential requirement for my business and this in turn has allowed me to focus on my customers and provide the same levels of service. So, to some extent I've based this book on my experiences and observations of all these businesses.

I've also studied marketing for a number of years for my own business. I belong to a small group of varied business owners who attend a two day, mastermind session once every 3 months. We take it in turns to sit in a hot seat for an hour and bare all our business problems and challenges. An excellent, if not slightly uncomfortable, opportunity to reflect on the big picture of my business. Everyone joins in with ideas on how to solve these challenges and ways to progress my business. By the time my session comes to an end, I have a detailed plan of action for the next three months. I also get a lot of insight into the challenges the other business owners have and how they're going to solve those. I find ideas that come out of others member's sessions can also benefit my business. All these businesses are growing rapidly and implementing the strategies I've learnt and detailed in this book.

It's so very easy to not see the wood for the trees when you're wrapped up in your own little world. All the day today problems of running a business get in the way. But I hope this book will help you get a clear idea of how to *grow* your business.

Some of the principles and strategies I'll share with you will make you feel uncomfortable. You may well think "I can't do that" or "The customers won't like that". You may not see the point, or relevance, in following some of the basic, initial exercises or of following the strategies through. But, they are all part of the overall plan to make your marketing a success and your business a success.

You'll also find my advice different from what you've heard from so called 'Marketing Gurus', 'Website Designers', 'SEO experts', and the like. Most things they come out with sound too good to be true and invariably they are!

Many of the tactics I cover will be familiar to you. The work you need to do on developing your strategies, how you can use these to your advantage when developing your tactics and what results you can expect from them, will probably be very new to you.

So, let's crack on......

PART 1

Grow Your Coffee Business Fast

What's the Key to it All?

HOLD UP!

Just before you dive into this book I'm going to ask you to do a little exercise.

Write down your strategies detailing how you're planning to, or how you are, growing your business.

Make it as detailed as you can.

Include everything.

Now, put is somewhere safe.

We'll look at it again later....

Chapter 1

How to Grow your Coffee Business Fast

I have been in business for a good few years and, like you, I wanted to grow my business and grow it fast. It's a sad fact that many businesses do exactly the opposite, decline and fail. Someone once said 'build it and they'll come' - I think they were referring to a flow of traffic to websites at the time - but the fact is 'they' won't. Customers won't necessarily just appear because you have arrived. This is true for all types of business. OK, you'll get some passers-by or be lucky enough to have a coffee shop in a very busy area that is devoid of other coffee shops, but generally you are going to have to market your business to grow it.

Despite planning and setting up a good business, many will fail in the first five years. This can be due to a lack of customers, lack of sales or low profits. All these things are fixable using the correct marketing strategies. Of course, you can just be unlucky and unforeseen circumstances may conspire against you. But mainly it's down to you, how you run your business and how you go about growing it.

Many business owners will look around for the magic 'thing' that will make their business a success. The one thing they can implement that will provide all the customers they want. Unfortunately, the magic thing doesn't exist, despite the promises of various gurus selling their advertising space or 'free' SEO packages. If there is one main ingredient, then it's hard work. This doesn't mean going at it like a bull in a china shop though. The real magic is in working smarter.

Having stated all that, there is one thing you can do to make your business really stand out. I'll reveal it later in the book because it helps to have an understanding of all the other principles and strategies first.

Sorry to keep you guessing but it will be worth the wait.

Most of your income and profits will come from your most loyal customers. However, customers have a limited life. By this I mean that customers come and go; some will move, some just change their habits and go elsewhere. To combat this, you'll have to attract new customers. This means marketing your business. In fact, no matter what business you are in, you are actually in the marketing business.

A coffee shop has to market their business. A garage has to market their business. A dentist has to market their business. A butcher has to market their business. Marketing is at the heart of everything you do, whether it's attracting new customers or keeping existing ones. Every interaction with any existing customer or new customer is a form of marketing. By interaction I mean everything, from the colour of the walls in your coffee shop, the complimentary biscuit on the side of the cup of coffee, the advert in the newspaper, it's all marketing. Even this book is a form of marketing for my business, as is the quality of the products I supply to my customers and the service I provide.

All your marketing activities are the key to growing your business.

I'll repeat that:

All your marketing activities are the key to growing your business.

But it goes further than this.

Marketing is not just about getting more customers through the door. As long as you are providing a good product and a good service then marketing your business properly will also allow you to position your business as the 'go to place'. It allows you to charge more for your products than your competitors and it will, in fact, make your competitors irrelevant. That may sound a bit of an exaggeration but in my business I've never worried about the competition. Every now and then a company will pop up selling coffee and machines to the trade at silly, cheap prices, trying to undercut the competition. They never last long. The reason they fail is because it's not about price, it's about quality products, quality service, but above all, relationships. It's the same for coffee shops, or any other business. You'll see why this is the case later.

So, marketing your business is the key to growth. But before we delve into that, there are some basic business principles that you need to be aware of. Although they are basic, and an understanding of them is fundamental to the success of your business, most business owners are blissfully unaware of them. Even if they are aware of them they either don't appreciate the importance of them or they choose to ignore them.

Knowing and applying these principles will put you at a huge advantage in your coffee business. The key word here is 'applying'. None of the information and strategies outlined in this book will help you grow your business if you don't take action to implement them. There are hundreds of self-help marketing and sales books that have been purchased and are now sitting on shelves gathering dust. They may or may not have been read, but the for the most part they have been forgotten.

Good intentions get you nowhere.

Knowing how to do it gets you nowhere.

It takes action, implementation and follow up to succeed.

Unfortunately, this book is going to be one of those that gets parked on the shelf because I know that only about 20% of the people who read this book will actually do anything constructive with it to grow their business. Further, I know that only around 4% will master their marketing properly.

How do I know this?

All will be revealed in Chapter 3.

SUMMARY

You are in the Marketing Business

Whatever business you are in, you're actually in the marketing business. Marketing is the key to your success.

There is No 'Magic Thing'

It's all just down to plain, simple hard work, the trick is to work smarter.

80 % of readers will do nothing after reading this book

Unfortunately, this is a fact and there is nothing I or anyone else can do about it.

Remember: Take Action

PART 2

Business Principles

The bits you ought to know before going into business.

Chapter 2

Most Business Owners Haven't Got a Clue

You read the title correctly, most owners have no idea about the basic principles that affect the day to day running of their business. The things that hold them back, why they haven't got enough time in the day, and why things can seem directionless. The following topics I'm going to cover may seem like they don't deserve a lot of consideration or that they don't even matter much, but they are vitally important and will govern your marketing and how fast you grow your business.

In the grand scheme of things, we're all allotted the same number of hours in a week. Some people manage to build empires with the time they have, while others don't even manage to fit the basics in. Most are somewhere in between, busy and surviving.

So, the key here is working smarter. To enable you to do that you need to understand and work on some basic principles. Take them seriously and spend some time working on them.

Your Aims and Aspirations

You have decided to read this book, so I'll take it that you're looking to grow your new or existing business. You obviously want a successful and busy establishment, maybe with the view to opening more outlets. As a minimum you need it to provide an income for you and your family, but if you are in business for yourself you also want to reap the extra rewards that you know are possible. Your company has to grow in order to provide these things.

So, the first question is what is your ultimate goal? Where do you want your business, your personal life and your financial position to be in 1 year, 5 years, 10 years from now? If you want to build up one outlet to give you a comfortable life style, that's fine. If you aspire to own a chain of outlets that's just as valid. But you need to know where you're going.

Many people like to have expensive cars or aim to live in a big house and the gurus of this world will tell you that you need to set these sorts of targets and goals in order to achieve success. You're supposed to have this overriding passion to own something or be someone. Perhaps you are like this. But many of us, and that includes me, are not. We're River People, a term coined by the late self-help expert Earl Nightingale. I have no over whelming ambition to own a Ferrari, for example. It would be nice but it's not that important to me. I am not particularly materialistic, but I like to have a good lifestyle. Having said that you still need to know where you want your business to go. You need to form a plan of where you're going and how you'll get there.

 I fly light aircraft, it's one of the things I like to do. I don't just jump in and set off with no idea of where I'm going or which route I'm going to follow to get there. I plan it, taking into account how high I can go, which areas I have to avoid, and who I have to talk to and deal with on the way.

Your business needs the same approach.

Where are you now? Where are you going? What route are you taking? And who do you deal with on the way?

So, sit down and work out your goals. There's a worksheet at www.gycsf.co.uk/plan to help you get your ideas together.

Branding

A note on branding. Your coffee shop or outlet will obviously have a name, but don't get carried away with trying to build a brand around it. Again, this is probably the opposite advice to what you've read before and heard on the Apprentice. I see it all the time in spam email from marketing gurus. 'Build your brand; focus on your brand; you've got to have a brand;' and so on. The truth is nobody cares about your brand, why this is will become apparent. Branding is fine for the large corporate companies but for a brand to become a household name takes millions of pounds' worth of advertising and years to achieve. As you will see later your marketing will be based on relationships not on a brand name.

The actor, Paul Hogan (he of Crocodile Dundee fame), did a series of Fosters Beer ads in the 80's and very funny they were too. They're on YouTube if you'd like to take a look at them. One of my favourites was towards the end of the series where he walks into a cocktail bar, hears the guy sitting at the bar order a fancy cocktail

where upon he makes a face, turns around and walks out. Fosters was not even mentioned. Very clever marketing but it must have cost a fortune to get the brand to this level.

So, branding works for the large corporates but not for small businesses. In general, nobody cares about your brand, what they care about is what you can do for them and how you can satisfy their wants and desires.

USP

So, forget the branding. But, as a business, you still need some way of standing out from the crowd. You need to develop a USP or Unique Selling Point. Something that makes your business different from all the run of the mill competition. Having a USP will also help when it comes to planning and executing your marketing, and help you to be clear about where you are positioning your business.

Your USP should answer the following question:

"Why should a customer buy from me in preference to one of my competitors?"

To come up with a USP start thinking along the lines of:

- What are you going to do that is different from your competitors?
- What can you offer your customers that will make you different?
- Can you theme your establishment in a way that stands out?
- What different service can you offer your customers?

Whatever you do, don't go down the route of just saying something is good or great. This is not a USP, so avoid phrases like:

'great quality coffee",

'great service'

'friendly staff'

'lovely ambience'

and so on.

You are in the coffee business and the quality of the coffee and the machines you use to produce it, the cleanliness of the surroundings your customers will experience, as well as the friendliness of the staff are the minimum requirements of your business. They are the basic standards you should be applying, not the unique parts of it. There is more on this subject in the last part of this book which covers coffee equipment, coffees and advice on providing a quality product.

For a USP you should be thinking along the lines of things that make you stand out from the crowd. This can, of course, include offering guarantees or even support for a charity.

Some examples of great USP's are:

A well-known pizza delivery company that offers to deliver your pizza within a certain time or its free.

Chocolates that melt in your mouth, not in your hand.

The sweet you can eat between meals without ruining your appetite.

Don't, however, make low prices the subject of your USP. Again, more on pricing later, but low prices will not help you grow your business. On the other hand, however, you can use high prices in your USP. Do you remember the ad selling a certain brand of beer as 'reassuringly expensive'?

Your USP doesn't have to be fixed for all time either, you can develop it and modify it as you go along. An example of how things change is that a few years ago one could use 'guaranteed next day delivery' as a USP, however, that has become the norm these days and is now standard procedure. You can also have more than one USP. This can be useful when you come to targeting different markets.

So, have a go at outlining some possible USPs, again there's a form at www.gycsf.co.uk/plan to help you.

Work ON your business, <u>not</u> IN your business

When you were planning your business and organising all the necessary stuff to set it up you were obviously working on the business. Once you open your coffee shop you will be spending time working in the business and getting everything running smoothly. I see many businesses where this becomes the norm, the owner is always present, often doing the mundane tasks that could be covered by anyone.

How many people do you know start a business because they want the freedom and essentially all they do is generate a job for themselves. You'll find they're working harder than they used to when they were employed and are gaining little benefit from working for themselves. This applies to many tradesmen, they leave a secure job in plumbing, say. Set up on their own and carry on plumbing, but now they have to do the sales, and marketing, as well as having all the headaches that come with regulations and paperwork. This happens in coffee shops too. People set up a coffee shop, then find themselves being a waiter or waitress but with the added responsibility of running a business.

What you should be doing is working ON your business, not IN your business. A minimum of 20% of your time and effort should be spent on marketing and growing your business. I know it's difficult. There are all sorts of demands on your time. Unexpected stuff happens, and the business has to keep running. So, the thing that suffers is usually the marketing, the one activity that is going to grow your business.

I've been there and done it, working IN my own business. Believe me it makes all the difference in the world when you start working ON your business.

SUMMARY

Write down your goals

Get a firm idea of where you want to be in business, personally and financially.

Come up with a USP

Summarise how your business is going to stand out from the crowd.

Basic Standards

Great products and great service are minimum requirements not unique features.

Branding

Your business needs a name but don't get carried away with excessive branding.

Remember: Work on your business, not in your business

Chapter 3

Business Principals

Before I get to the specifics of marketing and growing your business I'm going to consider businesses in general. You may consider that your coffee shop is a totally different business to any other type of business but it's not. A coffee shop, garage, dentist, butcher, or any business you care to name is there for one thing only and that's to make a profit. The tools are different, the products are different and the delivery is different but they all have the same end goal, to provide an income for the owner.

In the case of your business, that is your chosen method of making a profit and therefore a living. For a coffee shop, the main focus of your trade will be the coffee and the related products that you sell. You're relying on these to make your business a success and provide you with a good income. The coffee and coffee equipment will be a major factor in achieving this. As you go through this book you will see what relevance this also has on your positioning and marketing.

Before all that, I'll start with some basic numbers, the first being the 80/20 Principal or The Law of the Vital Few. As you will see this can have far reaching consequences for your business.

The 80/20 principal

You probably don't realise it but these two numbers can be applied to most things in your life. In 1906 a Swiss lecturer by the name of Vilfredo Pareto was carrying out some research into wealth. When studying the population of Italy, he discovered that 20% of the Italian population owned 80% of the land. Further research led him to discover that this pretty much holds true for every country in the world. Not only that, when you look deeper into statistics it turns out that this rule holds true for almost everything you want to consider.

For example:

- You wear 20% of the clothes you own 80% of the time.
- You spend 80% of your money on 20% of the items you buy.
- 80% of crimes are committed by 20% of criminals.
- You listen to 20% of your music collection 80% of the time
- 80% of this book was written in 20% of the time I allocated to it.

 It doesn't always work the way you think it will either. Before I started writing I assumed that 80% of this book would be written in the first 20% of the time I allocated to it. In fact, it was the other way around. 80% of the time was spent sorting ideas, the order to put them in, which logical way to present them, etc. Once the frame work was in place the content flowed surprisingly quickly. There's a lesson there – spend time on your planning – particularly your marketing planning.

The numbers are, of course, not always exactly 80/20 but often surprisingly close. They don't necessarily have to add up to exactly 100 either.

How does this affect your business and why is it important to know?

The effects on your business are:

- 80% of your revenue will come from 20% of your customers. Customers are not all equal.
- 80% of your sales will be made from 20% of the items you stock.
- 80% of your new customers will come from 20% of your marketing.
- 80% of any complaints you get will come from 20% of your customers
- 80% of any requests for something you don't stock will come from 20% of your customers.
- 80% of tasks will be completed in 20% of the time you allocated to them. That's why it's so difficult to get things finished sometimes.

Let's look at that last statement in a bit more detail because it has a direct effect on your productivity which you need to be aware of.

Take the fact that 80% of tasks you do will be achieved in 20% of the time allocated. Say you had 100 tasks to achieve in 100 hours. One per hour you might think. But the 80/20 principle states that 80 of those tasks will be achieved in 20% of the time, so 80 tasks will be completed in 20 hours. That's 4 tasks per hour or 1 every ¼ hour. The other 20 tasks will take 80 hours, that's 1 task every 4 hours.

This means that you were 16 times more efficient with the 80 tasks than you were with the other 20.

This is an inescapable fact, but you can do things to minimise it. Spend your time on the most effective tasks, drop some of the least effective ones or delegate them to someone who is free or better able to do it.

The big lesson here is to try and minimise the 20% of tasks which take up 80% of your time. You can't avoid it altogether but you can swing the numbers in your favour. Making you more efficient and able to achieve more in a given time.

Customer Value

The 80/20 principle applies to your customers too. As I said 20% of your customers will be responsible for 80% of your sales. In addition to this you will find that 20% of these customers will buy the most expensive products you have.

Having said that, a vital figure to know is your average customer value. Particularly for your regular customers. How much is each customer buying on average and how much profit is each customer worth to you. The reason this figure is important is so you can understand:

1. How many customers you need to make your business a success.

2. How much money you can afford to spend on your marketing to get a new customer.

Using a simplified example, let's look at your customer value. Say your average customer is a regular visitor for one year, then moves on. This customer spends £100 per month. So overall a customer is worth £1200 in sales of goodies. If your profit margin is 50% then you have made £600.

You now know that your average customer value is £600. Knowing this number will now allow you to decide how much you're willing to spend on getting a new customer. Even if it costs you £100 to get each new customer you are still going to be quids in.

Note, this is just an illustration, using simple numbers. The principle, though, is valid for all businesses.

Cost of Marketing

Most large companies will have a marketing budget. They spend up to a limit and that's it for the year. It's treated as a necessary evil and a set amount of money is allocated to it and that's that.

Most small businesses will pay for marketing as and when they can afford it. There will be an advert placed in the paper and then forgotten about.

Neither of these systems make any sense what so ever, they are both completely the wrong way to approach your marketing.

Take two coffee shops. The first places an advert in the local newspaper for £400. They see the income from sales go up in the next week by £250 and consider the ad a waste of time and money as they're now £150 out of pocket. No more ads are ever placed.

Coffee Shop number two does the same but this time they offer a loyalty card to every new customer who brings a copy of the advert with them. They discover that 20% of the new customers become regulars and as well as the £250 made in the first week they are also getting an extra return of £50 per week which they expect to get for the next year – the expected lifetime they have calculated for a customer. They run the advert again and after the initial burst of £250 find that another £50 income has been added to their weekly takings. Therefore, each ad has resulted in a total income of:

First week takings = £250

51 weeks of £50 takings = £2550

Total takings = £2800

The advert generated a total of £2800 in revenue or a return of £2400 for a £400 ad. How many times do you think they're going to repeat the advert?

Testing and ROI

The second coffee shop was testing and recording the results of their marketing. Their ROI or 'Return on Investment' was 600%. Every time they placed the advert they made more money. This is of course oversimplified but illustrates the importance of testing your marketing and quantifying the results.

That's why the budget model of marketing is wrong. If you're getting a good return on investment you continue investing, why would you stop? If you're not getting a good return, then you stop, reassess your options and try something else.

The other system, if you can call it a system, of just placing an advert and hoping that you'll get a good return doesn't work either. Without measuring it you have no idea of the true value of sales the advert has generated for you.

Although I've made it sound simple, that pesky 80/20 principle steps in again and you'll find that only 20% of your marketing efforts will produce 80% of the results you want. Yet another reason to test and measure the effects of a marketing campaign. If it's not working, stop, change it or try something else.

All forms of your marketing should be measurable by some means.

Trial and Error

Marketing is not an exact science, what works for one business won't necessarily work for another. As I stated earlier there is no magic 'thing'. You have to try things, see what works and what doesn't. Because you're now aware of the 80/20 principle you will know that 20% of your marketing effort will bring you 80% of the results. That means that 80% of your marketing efforts will fail or produce poor results. But don't get discouraged. That is 'knowledge', and you now know what doesn't work. You also know why it didn't work and that puts you ahead of the game. You're prepared for the 80% failure rate, unlike the majority of your competitors.

Let's go back to the advert in the last example. The second coffee shop found that the advert worked, so they ran it again. What they should do though is modify it a bit first. Say, try a new headline, monitor the results again and compare them to the previous advert. If it didn't work as well, go back to the old headline and change something else. Taking this approach, you can start to refine your message and learn what works best for your business in your location.

No one can tell you what will work best for your business and what won't, it all comes down to testing and monitoring the results.

The Majority Are Wrong

Strangely, most businesses in a given category all try to market their business in the same way.

- Tool and office supply companies all send a catalogue out in the post.

- Pizza Take Away companies all use door to door leafleting.

- And all Coffee Shops seem to be relying on a Facebook page to get 'liked'.

A well-respected marketer by the name of Earl Nightingale said words to the effect of, 'Look at what everybody else is doing, then do the opposite.' If all your competitors are advertising in the local newspaper, then let them get on with it and you do something different.

There was a time when I used to attend coffee related trade shows along with a host of other coffee companies. This resulted in all the potential customers being fought over by everybody. A pointless exercise. I stopped going to them and started going to regional catering shows where I was the only coffee company in attendance. There were fewer leads but the quality of them was far higher. It's interesting to note that the same companies are still plugging

away at the trade shows, I've heard more than one state that 'people expect to see us here' even if it's not cost effective. Pointless! Anyway, this neatly leads me onto another rule of business.

If it's not working, change it. You'll hear plenty of business gurus saying 'never give up' or 'keep plugging away at it until it works'. OK, so you have to give things your best shot but if it's not working, then change it.

The definition of insanity is to keep doing the same thing over and over again expecting to get a different result.

Growing your Business

Three. Yet another important number that has a direct influence on your growth.

There are only three ways to grow a business.

1.   Get more customers.

2.   Sell more to the customers you already have.

3.   Charge your customers more.

All these methods of growing your business involve marketing in one form or another. Remember you are actually in the marketing business.

The following few chapters will deal with these three ways to grow your business.

SUMMARY

80/20

Prioritise the activities you can do best, delegate those you can't.

Customer Value

Work out the value that each customer is worth on average. From this figure work out how much you are willing to spend on getting a new customer.

Test & Measure

Analyse your Return On Investment so you know what's working and, more importantly, what isn't.

There are 3 ways to grow a business

Get more customers, sell more to them and charge them more.

Remember: The Majority are wrong

PART 3

MARKETING

Chapter 4

Marketing is Simple

On the face of it, marketing is simple.

It's just a matter of getting the right message to the right person at the right time using the right method.

Simple. But while it may be simple, it certainly isn't always easy.

Some business owners do take the easy option. Stick a hand scribbled chalk board outside the door and sit back waiting for the customers to come flooding through the door. They won't be around for long.

 Mind you, I did see one that did intrigue me once. It was outside a small village pub. It read:

Cold Beer

Warm Food

Hot Wife

I didn't stop to find out if it was true or not, though I must admit I was tempted! I also reckon it would probably put off at least 50% of the potential customers as well! Interestingly, I never saw the sign again, though I often passed that way.

Marketing is the life blood of your business

Without marketing, you have no customers, without customers you have no sales, without sales you have no profit, and no profits means you very quickly have no business.

The concept of marketing may be simple but like everything else it needs to be planned in detail.

Marketing Plan

When you set up your coffee shop you went through a planning phase. The business plan was an important first step for your new venture. You needed one for the bank particularly if you were looking for any form of loan or a new bank account. You will have needed to provide this in some detail. Your business plan will have covered a few simple questions on the overall vision of your coffee shop with an idea of the type of operation you are planning. It will have included details of your proposed business, what products you are going to sell as well as research on the competition, etc. There were plenty of details of what's required for a business plan as well as templates, available on line. The main high street banks also had plenty of downloads and advice on completing them to help you.

Part of your business plan would have included your financial plan. This helped you keep track of where you were going and how you were progressing financially, and with a bit of luck kept your bank manager happy, if that's possible these days!

But, where's the marketing plan? It is essential to your business in every way.

As part of my research for this book I was looking through business plan templates that I found online. Several from banks and some from other companies, most addressed the marketing aspect with just two questions.

1 - How are you going to market your business?

2 - What method are you going to use?

Both, usually had boxes big enough for four or five words at best.

Strategies and Tactics

There are two parts to any marketing you do. Firstly, the strategies you develop, secondly the tactics you use to implement these strategies.

Don't confuse strategies with tactics.

The strategies you employ are the rules you follow and the methods you use to construct a marketing campaign. Strategies are fixed, they are rules that don't change with time, they are well tested and proven to work. They are, however, rarely used and the reason why most businesses are crap at their marketing.

The tactics are the different routes or mediums you use to get your message out there. These will change with technology and different areas of business. What works for a business in one area my not necessarily work for the same type of business in a different area. Tactics have to be tested and measured. Nobody can tell you what will work or won't work you have to find out for yourself.

Most business owners blindly set off using the tactics with little regard to an overall strategy. They'll often pay for, and rely on, a graphic design company to come up with something that's glossy and pretty. It looks the part but stands little chance of working. Just plonking stuff on platforms like Facebook, Instagram, Pinterest, etc., are just tactics. In fact, all these sites are simply variations of the same theme, just different ways of portraying the same content.

SUMMARY

Marketing is simple

The principles are simple, but not necessarily easy to implement.

Marketing Plan

Planning your marketing is an essential part of growing your business. Every bit as important as your financial or business plan.

Strategies

The well tested and fundamental rules of what works when it comes to marketing.

Tactics

The tactics are the various ways you can implement the strategies.

Remember: You are in the marketing business

Chapter 5

Grow your coffee shop Method 1

Getting More Customers

Probably the hardest part of your marketing to master. It's easier to market to existing customers but, as they have a limited lifetime, you will always need to find new ones.

This will be the longest section of this book and will cover a lot of the strategies that are applicable to all your marketing.

The Three M's

Yet another important number in business. The subject of marketing can be divided into what's called The 3 M's. They are:

Market - Who you are going to market to and what are you going to market to them.

Medium - What methods or mediums are you going to use to get your marketing message in front of them.

Message - What will the contents of your message be and how will you structure that message.

There is another one we could add - Motivation. This refers back to the goals you set earlier and the reason you're doing all this in the first place. Getting stuff done is an important part of your marketing success. It's not going to do itself. We'll look at some ways of dealing with this later on.

1 - Your Market

Who is Your Ideal Customer?

A simple example of where your marketing would be pointless would be trying to advertise tasty sausages to vegetarians, it would be a total waste of your time and money. You need to know who you are going to market to. So, you need to generate a picture of your ideal customer, an Avatar. This is the first step in your marketing process. Again, most business owners won't even consider this point and will think that any customer with a wallet or credit card is there ideal customer. It's no better to think that anyone who likes to drink coffee is your ideal customer either.

At first this may not seem to be that important but you cannot market to a customer without knowing, in your mind, who that perfect customer is. You need to write down all the facts you can about your Avatar, a complete description of that person. We tend to like people who have similar outlooks on life as ourselves, so you may see many of your own traits appearing in the description. Give them a name, I'm going to use Jo here (just because it's a convenient name that could be male or female, but I'll assume Jo is female for the purposes of this book).

Jo is your ideal customer, you need to know Jo's sex (as I said, female in this case), her age, her marital status, her likes and dislikes, what worries Jo, what area she lives in. etc. An important question is 'What does Jo want or desire'? Note, this is not the same as what she needs. People will pay for things they want as opposed to things they need. There are plenty of examples of this behaviour. You only have to look at television reports of people sitting outside pubs with a packet of cigarettes and a pint of beer complaining about not having enough money to live on. Strange that they can find enough to pay for the things they want as opposed to the things they really need. So, what are Jo's wants and desires?

What are Jo's problems. As well as satisfying desires and wants, people are also looking for solutions to their problems, is she a vegetarian with a lack of vegetarian options in other outlets? Is she a mother with no child friendly places about?

The more you know about Jo the better. There is an exercise at www.gycsf.co.uk/plan to help you out on this.

Why do you need an Avatar?

Because when you are engaged in any form of your marketing you need to have this person in mind. This is the person you are trying to attract into your business. The more specific you can be, the more targeted your marketing will be and the more appealing your message will be. You may think that this is too narrow a view but you cannot be all things to all people. You can't please all the people all the time.

Take the legal profession as an example. You often see an advertisement for a legal practice where all their services are lumped together in one piece of copy. They are trying to appeal to a range of people with different problems all at the same time. Trying to be everything to everybody. They would be far better off developing separate Avatars for each department and then displaying different adverts for people looking for, say, wills, conveyancing or divorces.

I know this approach works because I know the owner of a law firm that has adopted this approach. The enquiries they get now from local newspaper advertising far exceed what they used to generate from their combined message advertisement.

As I've just eluded to you can, of course, have more than one Avatar but any specific marketing piece should be directed to only one of them.

Who won't be your customer?

Another useful exercise is to describe the customer you don't want to attract to your business. You may wonder why you wouldn't want a customer, but there are people who can harm your business. Their general behaviour, complainers, the way they dress. It's your business so you decide who you do and don't want in it. Remember the good old 80/20 principal - you'll find that 80% of the complaints you get will come from 20% of your customers. Minimise them by not attracting them in the first place.

What are you marketing?

So, you've decided who you are marketing to. Now what are going to market to them? This goes far deeper than you may imagine. It's not just a product.

What does your Avatar want? Is she looking for somewhere cosy to meet friends or a place to get a take-away coffee? Remember, your customers aren't just going to appear because you're there. As I said earlier, customers are looking for something to solve a problem they have, or a want or desire. A need that they want to fulfil. What can you provide that fits in with your Avatars needs?

Marketing includes the décor of your establishment, the theme and the atmosphere you want to generate, how will this attract your Avatar?

As your business gets underway you will learn a lot about your market and what your customers actually want and desire. This may well differ from what you initially assumed they would want. Be prepared to change and adapt your concept, and re-visit your Avatar if necessary.

 One of my customers, who came from a bar and club background, set up an outlet where the wine bar was going to be the main focus, coffee was to be an add on during the day. As it turned out, the main focus became the coffee. The wine bar does well also, but the marketing and emphasis had to change to the coffee. Staff knowledge and training also had to be changed to reflect the shift.

Be prepared to adapt.

SUMMARY

Your Avatar

You need to know who your ideal customer is before you can market to them.

Not your Avatar

Just as important. You need to know who you don't want to attract into your business.

What are you Marketing

Have a clear idea of what you want to market to your Avatar.

Remember: Generating your Avatar is a vital step in your marketing strategy

2 – The Medium

You may think that the next step is to come up with your marketing message. But first you need to decide which medium or mediums you're going to use. You will need to craft a different message for, say, a press release than you will for a Facebook advert.

The medium is where you are going to use your tactics to market to your Avatar.

Now, from your Avatar you'll be able to tell me if she reads newspapers, uses Facebook, likes to wander around the shops, etc. Where will she see your message?

There are many varied ways of achieving this, more than you may think, so let's look at some examples.

You can divide these up into the 3 O's (it's getting silly this, 3 ways, 3 M's, 3 O's!) They are:

Offline

Online

Other

Offline

Pre-Opening Marketing

We'll start from the beginning and see what we can do to get customers through the door when you first open.

Before opening you need to market your coffee shop. If you're in a location where there isn't anything comparable then you won't have much trouble attracting your initial customers, people are naturally curious anyway, and you may open your doors to a rush, so be prepared. On the other-hand, if you're in a busy area with a fair bit of choice, people will tend to drift in at their convenience to try you out.

I supply machines and coffee to a company that has a chain of rural coffee shops and a different chain of inner city restaurants. The first coffee shop they set up was in a location where there was little competition. After they had been open for a couple of days I called in at lunch time to check how they were getting on with making the coffees. They prepare lunches in front of their customers and the operations manager was in the hot seat. As I walked through the door, past the queue of people waiting to get in, he took one

look at me, thrust a £20 note in my hand and asked me to go around the corner to Tesco's and buy him some avocados. Before I tripped off to the shop I asked if they had enough milk for all the coffee orders they were getting, they hadn't. I returned with the avocados and a load more milk.

In contrast, the restaurant they opened in London was in a very foodie orientated area. Having set up the coffee and coffee machine I decided that it would be fun to go and have a meal in the restaurant. It's a very busy area and I wondered whether we ought to book, even though they'd only been open a couple of days. I needn't have worried; it was very quiet. There's a lot of choice in that area and despite all the marketing they'd done it was a slow start. Even so, it has rapidly built into a very busy and successful restaurant.

As you can see, the initial response from potential customers can be very mixed. Unfortunately, you probably won't know if you're going to have a fast or a gentle start until you actually open and test the water. Whichever way it goes you need to be prepared. You need to train and organise your staff and have all the products ready to go. You can't ignore the fact, though, that you need to market your business before you open to get the best response possible. Let's look at some preopening activities you can employ.

The outside of your premises

This may sound obvious but if there is a big shop front, then make use of it. Include the name and when you're opening. You also need some reason for your potential customer to return when you do open and an introductory offer is a good idea, either for the first x number of customers or for a limited time. Also, include any website, Facebook, Instagram, etc. sites you may have set up for your business. How about a rack with some leaflets in it?

 I often see premises where we're installing a coffee machine and all the windows are blacked out. They're covered with either white paint or have large sheets of plain paper taped to them. Okay, it stops prying eyes from seeing all the messy work going on but you should also be using that area to get your message out to your potential customers.

Press Release

A good idea for a new start is to send a press release to local magazines and papers about your new or refurbished area opening soon. Editors are always on the lookout for a story to fill their papers. Build a personal aspect into it as well, you want your Avatar to connect with you. But more on your message in the next section. Even local radio stations have to fill time slots with local news of interest to their listeners, make your venture one of them.

Advertising

Press releases can be followed up with local newspaper adverts or leaflets. Many publications offer a service where you can have your leaflets inserted in them. Leaflets are probably a better way to go. They get noticed more than an advert on a page in a newspaper. The newspaper is only good for today, by tomorrow it will be out of date and the next copy will be available. Local shops often have boards where leaflets can be placed, better not to try the ones in the local competition though!

Give Aways

Give away coffee samples (or cake!)

In one coffee shop that I supplied, I did all the machine set up and staff training a few days before they opened. This left a few days for the

staff to practise their coffee making skills. The coffees they were making were produced in takeaway cups and a young lady stood in the doorway giving them away. She explained that the staff were practising their barista skills and, rather than throw the coffee away, they were giving it away free. Within 30 minutes' workers from an office block just up the road were calling in saying they'd heard that the coffee was really good and could they try one. They were busy from the day they opened.

Leaflet Drops

Door to door leaflet drops are a good idea, particularly with an introductory offer. There are plenty of companies out there who will arrange both the printing of your leaflets as well as the distribution of them. Some also provide a design and layout service as well, but make sure the principles outlined in the message section are followed.

Leaflets are a relatively cheap method of getting your message across and the distribution company can target the areas that you specify, the areas that your Avatar is likely to be found in.

After You're Open

Once you're open and you have your initial customer base you still need to carry on your marketing activities both internally and externally. Some of the previous ideas can still be used, occasional press releases cost nothing and can help promote new products or an event you're planning. Ongoing leaflet drops, with some method of measuring their effectiveness, are good.

 Another customer of mine runs a local pub/restaurant. He's always busy but I still get a leaflet through my door every 3 months. I have friends who wonder why he does it, after all he's always busy isn't he? Or is this why? Whichever, it keeps his establishment in mind. And it certainly works on me. When thinking of where to go with some friends who were visiting recently, there was the leaflet sitting on the side in the kitchen. "Oh! We haven't been there for a while, let's go there". And we did.

As the above illustrates you need to keep your customers aware of your presence. Just because you're busy today doesn't necessarily mean you'll always be busy. More than one busy business has faded away through a lack of marketing. Don't get complaisant, marketing your business and keeping customers aware of you must be an ongoing activity.

Contact details

One of the most useful things you can do is collect the contact details of your customers, particularly their email addresses. Of course, they're not necessarily just going to give these to you, you'll need to give them something in return. But once you have them it will enable you to market to them directly. This can include offers, information on new products or merely short stories about events and amusing things that have happened in your life as well as in the business. However, the main reason for collecting email addresses is so that you can build a relationship with your customers.

But, how do you get them?

There are many ways. You can be very straight forward and just ask for them, in return for a voucher perhaps or even the offer of an emailed voucher. A couple of other methods which can include a section for contact details are outlined below.

Always make it clear that email addresses may be used for your marketing, but make it equally clear that details will not be passed on to any third party, ever.

And don't ever pass them on!

Survey Cards

Use survey cards to give you some good feedback on how customers are finding your establishment. They are also very useful for obtaining your customer's email address. There are various ways of doing this, from just having an email section on the form to offering a weekly draw or a voucher which will be emailed to them. Questions on the survey cards can be whatever you like but try and keep it positive and aim to get your customers thinking in a positive way. For example, ask questions like 'What can we do to improve things? as opposed to "What didn't you like?

Loyalty Cards

This is a well-established method of getting repeat business from your customers. They are available from many small business printing companies, the same ones you can get your business cards from. Again, you can swap these in return for email addresses.

Use whatever method you can to obtain email addresses because, as you'll see, you can then build relationships with your customers. And growing your business is all about building these relationships.

Referrals

One of the best ways you can get more customers, is by referrals from your existing customers. You can just ask for them but a reward is always more appealing. I know of one outlet that used a system of 'rip cards'. They were cards that could be torn in half, the first half was for a new customer that had been referred with an offer on it. The second half was for the returning customer who also received a reward for the referral. Both parts of the card had a name on them so they could be matched up. I should imagine it took a bit of organising, but it worked.

Newsletter

Put a newsletter together, it costs pence to get them printed but will create interest for your customers. These can be available in the coffee shop, given out by staff or even posted to any customers you have an address for. I write a newsletter for my customers, it's a physical, 4 page, printed A4 size. Don't make it a sales leaflet though, the idea is to give your customers something of value.

I'm not sure where it came from but it's reckoned that a newsletter should be:

20% personal stuff, *your opinions on what's happening in the world or around you, what you've been up to, etc.*

40% business, *info on stuff, perhaps something educational. Recipes used in store, etc.*

20% entertainment, *puzzles, maybe with a prize draw at the end of the month for the first correct entry.*

20% business related, *customer of the month, stories from the coffee shop, etc.*

Menus

Be creative with your menus. It's not strictly a marketing method but it can still help to add interest and become a talking point. Include information on the products you're using, or use parts of it to put snippets in, similar to the bits you'd put in the newsletter, add a personal touch.

 I was in a restaurant in London where the menu was printed as a 4 sheet throw away newspaper. It had headlines and a little story about the wines, etc. It was a talking point and it works, well I tell people about it anyway!

Book

Write a book. Now, you're probably thinking how can I possibly write a book. Exactly what I used to think, but here's mine. A book doesn't have to be difficult.

 I have a friend who was in the beauty salon business, she used to write daily emails to her customers about all the stuff that happened in the salon. Eventually she got all these stories together, topped & tailed them and put them all in a book.

I recall a TV chef saying that every time she experimented with a recipe she just wrote it down. Again, eventually putting them all together and there was a book. It's not difficult it just takes some work and time.

So why a book? It positions you as a leader in your field. You are an author; therefore, you must know what you're talking about. You can sell it; you can give it away to your best customers; if you're trying to encourage a local company to use your outside catering facility you can use it as a business card. How many of your competitors will write a book? Even those competitors that know you've written one won't have the foggiest idea about why you've written it. But, even if they do have an idea why, they either won't see the value in it or won't be bothered to do it themselves.

Publishing is easy these days as well. You can self-publish. Many printing firms now have equipment that can produce 1 book, 50 books, 100 books, whatever you need. They're not expensive either. A small book may only be a couple of pounds to print, similar to some posh business cards I've seen.

The value of a book is, however, in the content. It may not cost much to print but it has taken work to put together and contains valuable information. Set a price that reflects this. There's an exercise at www.gycsf.co.uk/plan to help get some book writing ideas together.

Swing Sign

You can use a swing sign or menu board to promote products or menus or you could just have an amusing saying on it to catch a customer's eye. If you are writing it yourself make it neat, not like the hand scribbled one I mentioned earlier. If you can't write neatly then find someone who can. Careful here though because there may be rules on what you can and cannot display outside your coffee shop.

I once visited a customer who had a swing sign outside her coffee shop. It was all battered and in a sorry state. Apparently, the previous day one of her customers had tied her dog to it while she went in for a coffee. Unfortunately, the dog decided to follow her, pulled the sign over, scared itself silly and took off with the sign bouncing along behind it. Down the concourse and across the car park, the faster the dog went, the more noise the sign made, the faster the dog went. Both were eventually retrieved. I don't know what state the dog was in but the sign had certainly suffered.

Online

Everyone has an online presence now. From Websites to Facebook, Twitter, Instagram, Linked In and so on. An important note to remember here is that your Website is under your control unlike Social Media, the rules here are set by the owners of the media and they can change them whenever they like. And it is a fast changing environment, it's almost certainly changed since I wrote this. To some extent all these different systems are just different ways of doing the same thing, they just display things in different formats. New ones' pop up, old ones' fade away. In between these extremes, some become more fashionable. So, where do you start and how do you use it all?

Website

From my research, it seems that most coffee shops have abandoned the idea of a website and just concentrate on social media with pretty pictures of cakes with a caption, something like "come and try this" Remember, look around see what your competition is doing and do the opposite. I'm not saying that there's no place for Social Media, but a website is a must.

Customers expect to be able to find one. But what purpose should your website fulfil?

If someone is looking at your website, they are looking for information. Most websites are put together by web designers. They're called designers for a good reason. They have a passion for making a website look good as opposed to actually providing the information people are looking for. Most websites you see have a big picture at the top with some fancy bits popping up in it. All very arty and clever, but is it practical? If you use a web designer, pick the one who asks "What do you want your website to do?' Avoid the one who asks "What do you want your website to look like?"

A further consideration is that most web searches are now done on mobile devices. I recently heard one report stating that up to 70% of all searches are now carried out on mobile devices. So, having a desktop website that's also mobile friendly is becoming the wrong way to look at it. A website should now be designed for mobile and be desktop friendly.

Think about what you look for when visiting a website. Personally, I look at a coffee shop or restaurant site to see what time they're open, what the menu's like, where it is and how to contact them to book a table, or to book online.

It infuriates me when I can't find these things as I'm sure it does for many others. Large pictures of all the chefs' creations are all well and good, as are pictures of the surroundings generating an idea of the atmosphere, but make it easy for your potential customers to find the information they want

So, the first purpose of your website is to provide information for your potential or returning customers. The second purpose is to get those visitors details. As I said in the 'Offline' section, this is one of the most beneficial things you can do. There needs to be an offer or voucher code or something you are giving away in return for their details.

As a rule of thumb, you have 8 seconds to catch your potential customer's attention with the information they are after or a method of grabbing their details before they move onto another site.

8 seconds.

Make it count.

The most valuable part of your website is the top of the opening page, the bit you see before you start playing with the mouse to scroll down. Make sure your vital information and offer is in there.

Most people are lazy and will look at the first page and that's it. Don't get carried away developing the largest website in the world, it's a waste of time.

So, some website rules:

- Make the content of your website to the point.

- As with all your communications to your customers, make it easy for them to read. As a general rule, put black writing on a white background, avoid white on black or writing over a picture or graphics. Make it easy. Use a clear sans serif font, i.e. one without the squiggly bits, it's easier to read on a screen, and make it at least 12pt.

- Always use justified text with lines no more than 60 characters wide. Always indent the first line.

- Your copy should be about your customers. Talk about their problems, where can they go to meet friends? Where's a convenient place for lunch? That sort of thing and then tell them how you can solve their problem. It's as simple as that.

- Don't 'we' all over your copy! Don't use words like 'we do this',' we do that'. Your customers don't care. It's got to be about them. And never, never, ever start by saying 'Welcome to my / our website' Dive straight in and make it about them.

- Use the AIDA principle when writing your copy. This stands for Attention, Interest, Desire and Action. This is covered in more detail in the message section.

- All images should have a caption.

- All captions and headlines should be underneath any image. Most people will look at a picture or image first then reading gravity means they naturally progress down the page, missing a caption above a picture.

- Images should show products being used or consumed, don't just show a static picture of an object. Faces catch the attention as well. Studies have shown that female faces appeal to both men and women alike, more than male faces.

- You can and probably should use video. You don't need a 'professionally made, expensive, one though. Basic - homemade works very well. Video can be produced by anyone, and if you can make it fun then all the better.

 A friend of mine is a plumber. He's always loved playing with his video camera and posting the results on line. He's now got a reputation within the plumbing world for his home made 'how to' videos as well as his quirky, funny ones. His cat, George, appears in some of them as do his barbeques and all manner of random things. They're not professionally made. Yes, he edits them but you can still see the joins and cracks in them. He has, however, caught the attention of some large, well known, companies in the

plumbing, and building supplies trade who are now paying him to make their promotional videos. Preferring the real-life approach to the professional, flashy version.

- Every page of your website should have a purpose, a call to action or an offer to gain an email address.

- You will need a link to a privacy statement. Samples of privacy page text can be found online.

- You will need a link to an about page. Even this can be, and should be, written in a way that provides information on how you can be of benefit to your customer.

- Don't include links to Facebook pages, Twitter, etc. You've got your prospect onto your page, you've got their attention, you've got a good chance of getting their details. Don't give them the option of having somewhere else to go. If you do they'll wander off, won't return and the opportunity is lost.

- Make sure there is a mobile version of the site. As I said, more and more searches are being carried out on tablets and smart phones. Particularly if people are out & about and looking for the service you provide.

Your website can also host pages that aren't visible from the front page. These are landing pages. They're pages that you use as links from online adverts. If you do any form of online advertising on Facebook Google, etc. then you need a page on your webpage to send the traffic to, where you just focus on whatever the ad was for and capture their contact details. This page should have nowhere else for your potential customer to navigate to, though you will need to satisfy the rules of whoever you run your ad with. For example, at the time of writing, Google insist that you have a link to a privacy policy.

SEO

SEO, or Search Engine Optimisation, is pushed by many companies wanting you to spend your hard earned on getting them to somehow make sure you appear at the top of search engine lists.

Google and the like sell advertising, they're the listings at the top of the page when you search for something online. Basically, SEO companies are trying to beat Google at their own game.

 There was one account I heard of about an online retailer doing very nicely thank you from his online store, all supported by SEO to give him a 'front page' listing, Then Google changed

their algorithm and his listing just disappeared, shortly followed by his company. There was nothing he could do about it. Googles' site, Googles' rules.

Don't forget all these search engine sites and social media sites are owned by companies. They can change their rules as and when it pleases them to do so and if it buggers up your advertising or business there's nothing you can do about it.

Social Media

Social media is a good place to advertise. I'm not talking about your business or personal Facebook page, I'm talking about paid advertising. Your home page is a place where your existing customers can visit or can have links to. It's passive, your customer has to look at it and pick it out from all the other stuff that's posted on there. That's more to do with customer retention than getting new customers. 'Likes' on face book don't equal new or returning customers.

You'll have seen the ads that appear between posts on Facebook and advertising on these platforms can be good. Again, at the time of writing, (I have to keep saying that, because these things change rapidly) Facebook seems to be the place to advertise. You can pick your target market quite specifically to match your

Avatar. You can select ads to be displayed to users in a certain area, to a certain age range, to users with particular interests, etc.

Email Marketing

I've been going on and on about collecting email addresses throughout this section of the book and there's a very good reason for it. Email marketing is about the cheapest and easiest way you can reach your existing and potential customers. Consequently, this is one of the best ways you can grow your business. I keep hearing gurus saying email marketing is dead, it's all about social media now.

No, it isn't.

Not if you go about it in the correct way.

So, how should you go about it?

Remember you are trying to build a relationship with your customer, people buy from people and, just as you need to know your Avatar, your customer needs to know you.

Once you have an email address you can do several things with it, usually dependant on what you've offered in return for that information.

To start with, you could just email out your offer to the customer on an individual basis. But say you offered a series of recipes that you use in the coffee shop, this could very easily get out of hand if you're organising it manually. What you can do is set up an account with an email provider. Now, you can put an email sequence of the recipes into what's called an autoresponder. An autoresponder holds the sequence of emails that you have prewritten on your chosen subject. These can then be programmed to be sent out at a set time interval, daily or every Friday at a set time, for example. Once you enter the details of a customer the sequence starts. You can add further email addresses and, each time you do, the new customer starts receiving the sequence of emails. There are several companies offering this type of service, some are free to start with, while others are paid sites. Examples of companies supplying this service are Mailchimp, Aweber, and Infusionsoft. Some are more complex than others, so look around to see what would suit you best.

Another way of getting customers on your email list is directly from your marketing. This is where it can get very clever because it can be completely automated. Take this sequence for example:

You have an advert on Facebook, perhaps for a sequence of weekly vouchers.

Someone clicks on the advert; this takes them to the landing page on your website.

Your landing page includes a sign-up box that you've generated in say, Mailchimp.

They see your offer on the landing page, pop their details in the box and press the button to get the offer.

This immediately puts their details into your email sequence in Mailchimp.

You've set your sequence in Mailchimp to send an email immediately, thanking them for signing up for the vouchers and the first one will be sent out soon.

You've set the first voucher to go out at 10 am the following day and it is duly sent.

A week later the second voucher is emailed out, a week later the third and so on.

All automatically.

But now the real business of growing your business can start. You've got the email addresses; the customers have gone through the initial sequence that you used to get them. So, what now?

You now move the email addresses to your standard list, again with most autoresponders this can happen automatically. The email addresses on this list will receive your regular, conversational emails. How regular is regular you may ask.

Daily.

Send daily emails.

If you can't manage daily make it at least 3 or 4 times a week. Most marketing gurus will tell you that sending daily emails is far too many, some even baulk at weekly emails. You'll be told that you are spamming people, you'll annoy people and instead of growing your business it will have the opposite effect.

Believe me, it won't. But you do have to go about it in the correct way.

 I personally know several business owners that do just this, every day, day in day out, and if they miss a day they get emails asking them if they're OK because the expected email didn't arrive.

So, the rules for sending daily emails:

- They have to be personal, by that I mean you are writing them as you would write a letter to a friend.

- You write as if you are talking to one person. Remember your Avatar? Include their name in the text. The email software will put this in for you.

- They are plain text. No fancy templates. No pictures. No logo. As I said, just like a letter to a friend.

- They are sent from you, personally. When the customer sees your email in their inbox the "From" is just your name. Not a company name, not a brand name, not a shop name.

- Now you need a headline. The only purpose of a headline is to get your reader to read the first line of your email. Make it intriguing, but whatever headline you come up with make sure you deliver on it.

An example of what not to do:

She looked Sexy

Now that I've got your attention, I want to let you know about our new menu....

In this example the subject bares no relation to the content. OK it may have got your reader to read the first line but they feel cheated, unsubscribe and that's the last you'll see of them.

An example from one of my emails was:

The hammer went through the ceiling.

I'd had enough.

The room was always cold.

'Oh! No. Here we go again" cried Cecelia as I started to rip the ceiling down.

There was no insulation in the flat roof above the dining room, so the ceiling had to come down.

This followed on with a story about my exploits in fitting insulation and replacing the ceiling, but I delivered on the headline, the reader got an explanation of that headline. I'll refer to this example again in the following rules:

- As a general rule, make the first three lines short, gradually getting longer. It leads the reader into the rest of the email.

- In the above example, I explained the headline straight away. I could have made the second line: *'I'll explain in a minute.'* And come back to it later in the email, that works OK, as long as you do come back to it!

- Give a story continuity from one email to the next, so the reader is keen to get the next one. The next one in my sequence was about me turning grey. Just the dust from rubbing down the plaster joints.

- If a particular story has come to an end then mention something else, some other event or a hint about the next story and say something like: *'I'll explain tomorrow.'*

- Make the content conversational on any subject you like. Don't make it all rosy either. If you've cocked something up, write an email about it; had a bad day, share your experience. People like the fact that you're just as fallible as they are. Don't make them all work related either. My ceiling was nothing to do with coffee or coffee machines. You can make it about some TV program, a news item or your opinion on something. Anything.

- Remember you're aiming to attract your Avatar to you, the customer you want in your business. Don't worry about upsetting or distancing yourself from the people you don't want to deal with in your business.

- Always have a postscript ('p.s.')

- Always have a call to action, preferably in the text and repeated in the p.s. It can be related to the topic you've been writing about or completely separate. Use linking phrases like "By the way…."

- If you want to show a picture of something or a video put a link in the text. This does two things. Firstly, it keeps your text easy to read with no distraction. Secondly, it trains your customer to click a link when you tell them to. On that note, people like to be told what to do, it removes the decision process from them. More on that a little later.

- Use the same text rules as you did for your website.

- Always make sure there's an unsubscribe link at the bottom of the email.

So, whatever mix of marketing tactics you choose make sure email marketing is in there.

Keep copies of your emails as well. You can collate them, top and tail them and there's your book. Just as my friend did. How about "The hazards of being a Coffee Shop Owner – A series of short stories'. You get the idea?

I'll just add a couple of notes on statistics. Once you start emailing you will find that you'll get some unsubscribes. This is not necessarily a bad thing though. If you've pitched your message correctly, then they're probably the ones you don't want as customers. They're also the ones that are least likely to buy from you. It's called polarisation, and there's more about that later.

Don't worry about 'click through rate' either. This is a statistic available from your email service provider. They can measure how many of your emails were opened. Many emails are read in the preview section rather than being opened, and these don't show up in the figures. So, don't worry about them.

Other

As I explained in the introduction, every interaction with a customer is a form of marketing or an opportunity to market to them. The décor and the atmosphere all help to market your business, as do your staff.

Staff

Your staff will be the main interaction your customers will have with your business. You are relying on them to represent you and provide a great experience for your customers.

You need to be clear what you expect from them when welcoming a customer, a cheery 'Good Morning, how are you today?' or whatever you decide it should be. It's the little things that can make all the difference here.

The best way to go about this is to have a rule book and process manual. This is not a stand-alone marketing tactic as such, but your business should be run on the basis of formal processes.

Processes

Systemise your business. If the way staff interact with customers is detailed in the process manual, then they know what standards have to be met. If they don't adhere to them then you have a firm basis for dealing with the problem.

You should have a manual of every process in your business. From opening in the morning to shutting up shop at night.

The first benefit of such a manual is that everybody knows where to find out how to do things.

Secondly, an operational manual will greatly increase the value of your business should you wish to sell it.

You can create such a manual over time, say one process per day. Set out a sheet, title, date, who it effects then add the steps you need to complete the process.

 I've done this in my own business. An example is the process to fill in an FCA, Financial Conduct Authority, return. I'm required to do this once a year because I offer leasing as a machine purchase option. As you can imagine, it's not straight forward. The first time I had to submit the forms I documented each step, including screen shots of the relevant FCA site pages. So,

next year I or anybody else can check the process and complete the forms easily. (Assuming the FCA don't change them!)

Document your business processes and re-visit them regularly to make sure they're still up to date.

A great book on this subject is 'Work the System' by Sam Carpenter. There's a website too, www.workthesystem.com.

Check it out.

SUMMARY

Customer Details

The most valuable information you can collect is your customer contact details. Email addresses in particular.

Relationships

Building personal relationships with your customers is the key to growing your business.

Email

Probably the best way to promote yourself, promote your business and grow.

Remember: Become the Expert to your customers

3 - The Message

This is your sales script. Your message to your potential customers. We'll look at the content you need to include, and what to avoid.

By now you should know:

Who you are selling to.

What you are selling to them.

Which tactics you are planning to use.

But:

When do you sell to them?

And:

How do you sell to them?

When do you sell to them?

The answer is - **all the time**.

Your potential customer will buy when they're ready to buy, and when they're ready to buy then your name or what you're offering has to be in the forefront of their minds. Gone are the days when one coffee shop or one butcher or one of anything was the only choice. Now the consumer has a huge choice available to them for almost anything they desire. You have to make sure your potential customer has you in mind when they're ready to buy.

The problem is that you cannot possibly know when this is going to be, so your marketing has to reflect this.

This is why sending daily emails can be so valuable to you. Being part of your customers' life, whether they realise it or not, will keep you in mind. This then has the power to revolutionise your sales and your business.

So, market to them relentlessly. Until they die or tell you to stop.

How do you sell to them?

More often than not, an advert for any sort of business will display the name of the establishment in large letters at the top along with their logo. Then there will be a picture of a static object with some offer of a discount. These ads are usually put together by a graphic designer, keen to show off their skills and fancy artwork.

What's wrong with this? Well, to start with people don't care about:

Your brand

Your logo

Your Name

Your Products

What you like

What you're passionate about

How long you've been in business

How much you earn

We've all seen ads and websites saying things like '…. we've been in business for 5 years and are passionate about our pretty little widgets…'

Nobody cares how long you've been in business or how passionate you are about little widgets.

What they do care about is what you can do for them. How you can solve a problem they have. It's all about them, not you. So, all your communications with your customer or potential customers must address their needs. So rather than a graphic designer you're better off using a copy writer. But, why not do it yourself? You may find it difficult to start with but, like everything it gets easier with practice.

If you are planning to write your own copy then here are some rules to help you along.

Firstly, I'm going to recommend a book, it's the result of research into what works and what doesn't when it comes to designing the look of your copy. It's called 'Type and Layout' by Colin Wheildon, you can find it on Amazon. It's not a huge book but there's loads of useful stuff in it.

The structure of your message should always follow the AIDA principle in **every** communication you have with your customer. You may well have heard of it. It's been around for a long time and the reason for that is, it works.

The AIDA Principal

If you've not come across this before it stands for:

Attention - Interest - Desire - Action

Let's look at each of these in turn.

Attention - The first job of any sales piece is to grab the attention of the reader. A compelling headline that will make them want to read on, just like the title of your emails did. Again, it must be relevant to the rest of the message.

Interest - Having gained their attention, you now have to spark their interest by backing up the headline.

Desire - Here's where you get the reader hooked into wanting your offer, or product.

Action - Tell your reader what you want them to do and how to do it.

These are not necessarily separate elements of your copy. It should flow from one to another but should follow this logical pattern.

As well as these four sections of your copy there are 12 elements it should include as well.

1. A compelling headline
2. A compelling first line
3. A compelling body copy
4. Logically Progressive subheadings
5. A genuine reason for writing
6. One or More Pictures with a caption
7. An offer
8. A reason to respond now
9. A method of responding
10. A guarantee
11. Post-scripts
12. Testimonials

Taking these one at a time:

A compelling headline.

This is to get the customers attention and get them to read the first line of your copy.

A compelling first line.

The purpose here is to lead the reader into the rest of the text.

A compelling body copy

There are various ways of doing this. For example, you can lead your reader to realise the problem they have got and then provide the solution. Perhaps get the taste buds flowing by describing a menu then revealing when it's available.

Logically Progressive subheadings

This probably sound obvious, but you need to plan the flow of your copy.

A genuine reason for writing

You need a firm reason for writing, other than just selling a product. A forthcoming event or holiday for example. Again, think of your readers wants or problems and how you can help solve them.

One or More Pictures with a caption

A picture can tell a lot about your offer, but make it dynamic, someone enjoying coffee, for example, as opposed to just a boring picture of a cup of coffee. Always include a caption under the picture and put the picture at the top of your publication. People tend to look at pictures first then move down the page. It's termed 'reading gravity'.

An offer

Always include an offer. If there's no offer then there's no incentive to respond to the advert.

A reason to respond now

Again, there must be a reason to respond to the offer, an open-ended offer is useless. Use a time limited or scarcity factor to encourage a response.

A method of responding

There's a well-known story of a company sending out hundreds of postcards, during a sales campaign, and forgetting to add any method of responding, no phone number, no address, nothing. Decide how you want people to respond and make it easy for them to do so.

A guarantee

You should include a great guarantee. Don't be scared of adding one. Very few people will ever abuse it. A guarantee takes the risk element away from the customer.

 A friend of mine wrote a book and offered a money back guarantee if a customer didn't like it, for whatever reason. You didn't even have to return the book. He's sold loads and never once had a refund request.

Post-scripts

Add a p.s. at the bottom with a repeat of the offer in it, even if readers skim through the main copy they will usually read the p.s. at the bottom.

Testimonials

If you have any testimonials for the item you're promoting, make sure you add them in. Testimonials add weight to your offer.

SUMMARY

When do you sell?

All the time. Customers buy when they're ready to buy, not when you're ready to sell to them.

Why do customers buy?

Customers care about what you can do for them, how you can satisfy their desires and fulfil their needs.

Your massage

Make your message compelling and aimed at your Avatar.

AIDA

Attention, Interest, Desire, Action. Include all these elements in any interaction with your customers.

Remember: Sell constantly

Chapter 6

Grow your coffee shop Method 2

Sell more to your customers

The only two strategies for selling more to your customers are, one, sell more to them each time they visit, and two, encourage them to visit more often. Preferably both. There is actually a third, you could sell to them externally, for example, a pack of goodies delivered once a month to their home, but we'll concentrate on your coffee shop here.

Selling more per visit

I'll just go through some tactics you can use here, but don't forget to apply all the marketing strategies that we've covered to them.

Staff training

I mentioned earlier that your staff are your representatives and as such should interact with the customers as you want them to. But, your staff must be knowledgeable about the products they're selling as well. It sounds obvious but so many aren't. Your staff are your sales team, if they don't know what they're selling, how can they possibly sell it effectively?

I like a pint of real ale occasionally and our local pub is pretty good at featuring guest ales. Most seem to have quirky or even silly names that don't give much away as far as what's going to end up in the glass. I mean, what's 'Nelsons Revenge', 'Gardener's Delight' or 'Leg Spreader' going to taste like? I guess the last one's probably a bit on the strong side! But there's no clue to the taste. Ask the staff what they taste like and invariably you get the 'I don't know' sometimes followed by 'people seem to

like this one'. How easy would it be to give the staff an outline of what the drinks are like, it could be as simple as adding a small note on the back of the beer pump handle. Something like 'light citrus flavour, medium strength" or 'dark malty, full bodied' but, no, they haven't a clue. It's not all bad though, I can usually get a free sample of each to taste but I shouldn't have to.

That's a simple example, but often a common problem when it comes to the more complicated items being sold. Your staff need to know as much as possible about the items they're selling. This is even more crucial for the following tactics.

Upselling

Your team should always be looking for the upsell and you need to put a list of complimentary items together for them to sell. From a piece of cake that will best compliment the coffee, to the wine that goes with a certain dish. Don't get too pushy though, nobody likes a pushy sale. It should be more of a recommendation or suggestion. You can also back it up with time limited offers. Changing the upsell options every now and then will help to keep things fresh and interesting for your customers. And, if one becomes very popular add it into the permanent menu.

Bundle stuff

A form of upselling I guess. Bundle stuff together. Put meal deals together or bundled take-away offers. It's another way of adding more perceived value to a sale.

New Items

Keep things fresh. Add new items regularly. Throughout the year you can offer a different flavoured coffee of the month to compliment your standard range, or a speciality sandwich of the month, etc. When it comes to seasonal events you can have a seasonal offering of some sort or a change of menu. You can and should be creative here, most outlets will put up decorations for seasonal events, some will have a small seasonal offering but most will just offer the standard range that's always available. Again, most will only embrace Christmas but as well as the obvious other events like Easter and Halloween, there's any number of excuses you could use to be seasonal – Midsummer, Burns night, etc.

A couple of my customers do a roaring trade in Christmas Hampers, taking orders in November to give themselves time to prepare them. They offer a range of sizes and prices and there's great scope here for some expensive, top-end, items.

Retail shelf.

Why not have a retail shelf for selling items. They could be versions of what you already sell or different items. Several of my customers do this. A couple actually have a whole wall of shelving displaying items for sale.

High Priced Items

Remember the 80/20 principle predicts that a small proportion of your customers will buy your most expensive offering. Always have a top-end product, even one that you think nobody will ever pay that amount for. You will be surprised.

My 'top of the range' coffee machines are nearly double the price of the standard professional model. I don't sell many of them but they do sell. Not only that but they're often the easiest sale. The customer has already decided that they're going to buy the best beforehand.

Layout of your Coffee Shop

This may not seem so obvious but where you locate your equipment can influence what your customer buys. Take the coffee machine for example. If it's located in full view of the customers it will help sell the coffee. If it's hidden away where nobody can see it then it's not obvious what you're producing and how good it may be. So, when planning your coffee shop pay attention to the layout and which parts you want the customers to be able to observe easily. If you can make some theatre out of a process, then show it off.

Get your Customers to visit more often

The second way to sell more to your customers is to get them to visit more often.

There are various tactics you can use for this, most of which we've already covered, loyalty cards for example. I'll just add the following though.

Limited Offer

This is something you can use in a lot of your marketing. In fact, all offers need a limit whether it's for use by a certain date or for a certain event. There must be a reason to get the customer to respond, so any offer or voucher needs a time limit. Try not to make it too long though, you want the customer to take action before they forget about it.

Scarcity is another way of limiting a promotion, 'when it's gone it's gone' or 'while stocks last'.

Special one off events will attract a number of customers and get them to return. A themed evening or wine tastings perhaps, even coffee tastings.

Continuity System

The greater profits are always in some form of continuity system. The loyalty cards mentioned earlier are such a system. There are other various ways of addressing this, from setting up a lunch club or coffee club to some form of monthly prepaid offer.

This may take some setting up but is worth investigating and testing.

SUMMARY

Training

Your staff are your sales team. Make sure they are knowledgeable about your products.

Limited Offers

Any offer should have a limit, either a time restraint or a quantity restraint.

Top End

Always have a high-end offering. There are a small percentage of customers who will buy the most expensive items.

Continuity

Test ways of getting the customer to buy more often.

Remember: Keep things Fresh

Chapter 7

Grow your coffee Shop Method 3

Charge your customers more.

Premium Positioning

Having followed the first two methods of growing your business. You can now develop the third method.

You have followed your marketing plan.

You have used the correct strategies along with the right tactics to build a loyal customer base.

This all goes hand in hand with your positioning.

You have now positioned yourself as the leader in your field, the expert and the person they have got to know. Therefore, your establishment has become 'the place' to go to.

Expert status

How do know you are the expert in your field? The answer is, you declare yourself the expert. Nobody needs to give you permission. It's your business. You set the rules, you attract the customers you want, you set the standards. Don't let anyone else dictate to you.

The One Thing

In the first part of this book I said that there was one thing you could do to make your business really stand out.

Have you realised what it is yet?

Being the expert makes you stand out from the crowd but you can fine tune that. Instead of just becoming a general expert in your coffee business, you can and should become known as the expert for one thing and one thing only. The 'one thing' will get you recognised and everything else will piggyback on the strength of that.

 While visiting San Francisco a few years ago we were told by friends to make sure we visited a certain coffee shop. It's called the Buena Vista Café and they're famously known as the experts at making amazing Irish Coffees. And they were. Not only did they taste fantastic but the way they were making them was well worth watching too. Search for Buena Vista Irish Coffee on YouTube and have a look. The Irish Coffees were the draw but the place was rammed serving lunches and sandwiches as well.

What could you be the expert at?

Irish Coffees?

Speciality Cappuccinos?

Pies?

If you can develop a niche, and become well known for it, you can market that and build a reputation based on it. Don't ignore all the other parts of your business though, they are just as important, but the niche will be the primary draw to get the customers through the door. It will take hard work and time to develop but when you do crack it, it will stand you head and shoulders above any competition. It doesn't have to even be food or drink based, have you wondered why I wrote this book? Writing a book will make you stand out as well. How many of your competitors will do that? They won't even understand why you've done it or see the value in it. **Your competition has become irrelevant.**

Polarisation

You should polarise your business and marketing by putting your personality on it. Polarisation is the term used to describe a certain position you take and stick with. For example, if you have a strong opinion on a form of politics you will tend to attract people who agree with you while repelling those that don't.

Your coffee shop for example may play jazz music in the background, those that love it will be attracted to you, those that don't will go elsewhere. Again, most coffee shop owners won't do this.

Your business – your rules.

Positioning and polarisation have now taken us full circle - back to your USP. You now build your business based on your expert status.

Premium Pricing

Increase your prices

Almost everybody I talk to is loath to do this. Let me ask you a question. How did you set your prices in the first place or how are you planning to set them?

Let me take a guess.

You've checked out all the local coffee shops to see how much they charge and then you've set your prices somewhere around the average. Am I right?

I'll let you into a little secret, my busiest and most successful customers charge the most for their products. Strange that!

Do People Buy on Price?

Simple answer.

No.

If they did we would all be driving around in the cheapest car available, taking cheap holidays, drinking the cheapest wine. Buying products is an emotional thing not one based on logic. As long as the customer sees the value in something they will be willing to pay for it. Only about 5% of people buy on price, and these are probably the hardest ones to satisfy, the ones you don't want in your business anyway. That leaves a whopping 95% of customers who aren't price conscious. And, out of that group you'll find that about 5% of them will buy your most expensive offering. As I said earlier, you should have some top-end products, you'll be losing out if you don't.

Price Elasticity

Pricing, just like everything else in your marketing and business, must be tested. Put your prices up by 10% and test the reaction. I can guarantee hardly anyone will notice. If they do, they may make some casual comment about it and that'll be that. A month later put them up another 10% and keep doing this until you start getting some price resistance. Now you know what your customer base are prepared to pay for your products and service. You can now leave the prices as they are or go back to the last price that everybody was happy with.

Pricing is elastic, you can't possibly know what your customers are willing to pay until you test it.

Offers and Discounts

Discounting is generally not a good idea. It has its place as a tool for attracting new customers, where you can offer discount tokens for a coffee, say in your advertising.

A far better way to present an offer is to add value to the sale. There's a number of ways you can do this, for example 'buy 1 get 1 free', which you often see in supermarkets, or add a freebie with the initial purchase. You may think this is the same as discounting but there's a big difference, three things are happening here:

1 The customer sees the value in the offer.

2 Because you charge the correct price for the main item the customer is accepting that this is the price you charge for that item.

3 They will happily accept this price the next time they purchase the item without the offer.

Quality, Service, Price

There is a saying that you can have Great Quality, Great Service and Low Prices, BUT, you can't have all three.

The following quote explains nicely:

"It's unwise to pay too much, but it's worse to pay too little. When you pay too much, you lose a little money - that's all. When you pay too little, you sometimes lose everything, because the thing you bought was incapable of doing the thing it was bought to do. The common law of business balance prohibits paying a little and getting a lot - it can't be done. If you deal with the lowest bidder, it is well to add something for the risk you run, and if you do that you will have enough to pay for something better."

*— **John Ruskin***

Or simply: Buy cheap, Buy twice!

Great products and great service are the minimum requirements of your business. Introduce great products and provide a great service and your customers will happily pay for the experience.

Pricing and Profit

Let's look at your pricing and see the effect it has on your profits. Say a table of customers end up with a bill of £100 and your profit on that is £30. You decide to offer a 10% discount to be cheaper than Bob's Butty Bar down the road. Their bill now comes to £90 and your profit is now £20, that's a reduction of 33.3% in profit. But if you've positioned your business such that you can increase your prices by 10%, which any customers worth having won't notice or worry about, then your profit becomes £40. That's an increase in profit of 33.3%. And the overall effect of increasing your price by 10%, as opposed to discounting by 10% means your profit is doubled from £20 to £40, a 100% difference. Now if one or two customers decide they don't want to pay the increase, that's fine. You will have more than covered the cost of losing a couple of price buyers.

Pricing Reviews

Pricing is something that you need to keep on top of. Prices of stock can creep up without you noticing. Inflation is another factor which will reduce your profitability over time. Not increasing your prices when costs increase will not only cut your profits it will inevitably lead to your downfall. As we've just seen a small monetary change can mean large percentage changes in profit for you.

Another quote for you:

Turnover is vanity, profit is sanity.

Make sure you keep sane.

SUMMARY

Status

Position yourself as the expert in your field.

People and prices

Most people don't buy on price. Their emotions rule the purse strings.

Discounting

Discounting hits your profits hard. Only use it when necessary or for getting new customers.

Pricing

Pricing is elastic, test it to see where you should be setting the bar.

Remember: Profit is sanity

Chapter 8

Putting it all together

Building a successful business involves hard work and consistent attention to the details of marketing. By putting all the factors in place that I've outlined you will have a marketing plan that will grow your business. A plan that will get new customers into your business, keep them there and make a good profit for you. To help you sort out your marketing there is a download at www.gycsf.co.uk/plan

JFDI

A term often used in business circles, I don't mean to shock you but: -

Just F***ing Do It.

Easier said than done, I know, but that's the only way any of this is going to work. At the beginning of this book I said that only 20% of readers will actually do anything constructive after reading it. I hope you are in that 20% and if you are, here's a couple of tips to help you along.

Time Management

There are many books and loads of rubbish written about time management but you can go a long way to improving yours by doing a couple of simple exercises.

Firstly, what are you doing with your days now? Get a sheet of paper and write down the time you start and finish any activity you carry out. Not just '08.00 – 13.00 worked in the shop', but try to break it down to individual tasks and activities.

Do this for a week, then analyse what you've been doing.

In true 80/20 fashion, you'll find that you could have delegated or cut out most of the tasks you were doing. Sort out the important stuff, off-load the rest.

Secondly, one of the biggest wastes of your time will be interruptions, queries from staff, phone calls, emails, checking Facebook, etc. This is easily combatted by putting some rules in place. Things like:

Get staff to make decisions instead of relying on you, unless it's urgent. Have a set time for non-urgent staff queries.

Turn the phone off, or put it on silent.

Check emails and social media twice per day at a set time – say 11am and 4pm.

Pomodoro

A great little app you can download for your smartphone is Pomodoro or Focus Keeper. You set work periods of, say, 25minutes followed by a 5 minute break. This is repeated for 4 cycles, then you get a 30 minute break. An alarm goes off to notify you when time's up. Somehow you can work better knowing there is a time limit and the reward of a break coming up. I'm always amazed at how fast 25 minutes goes by when I'm working but I find taking a break keeps me fresh.

Writing

Many people have a problem with writing, I certainly know the feeling! Do you look at a blank piece of paper and wonder where to start? Perhaps you don't think you can write. Here's a couple of exercises to help get you going:

Firstly, a simple one. If you are stuck and have the legendary 'writers block' just start rambling, even write down things like 'I have no idea what I'm going to write about, could be ……' You'll find it just gets you going.

A good little exercise if you aren't confident in your ability to write well is this. (Make sure you read all the rules before you start though).

1   Pick 3 random words. For this exercise use Pidgeon, Bucket, Microphone.

2   Set the timer on your phone for 5 minutes. Put it where you can't see it counting down.

3   Start writing and continue as fast as you can, don't worry about typos, grammar, or whether

it's making sense or not. Don't stop until the timer goes off.

4   The first sentence must contain all three of the random words, and one of the random words must be the first word of this sentence.

When you've finished, go back and read what you've written, you'll be surprised at how much sense it does make. Now you can check the spelling, grammar and punctuation.

Give it a go.

The Vital Factors

Of course, none of your marketing efforts are going to be any use what so ever if you don't give your customer a quality product. The products and service you provide should be excellent at all times. As I keep saying, this is a minimum requirement of your business and shouldn't be something special. In fact, your whole focus should be to provide your customer with a memorable experience.

Adding a few small touches can make all the difference. From a staff members smile to the little biscuit on the side of the coffee cup.

One of the biggest factors is consistency. There are no hard and fast rules as to how you prepare any particular dish, coffee, or anything else. Your customer will, however, expect the same thing next time they order it. This means consistent products as well as staff training to make sure they are all singing from the same hymn sheet.

Quality and consistency should be at the heart of everything you do.

Quality Equipment & Ingredients

Offering a quality product comes down to the quality of the equipment you're using as well as the quality of the ingredients you're buying and, of course, the quality of the training that your staff have been given…..

…..which, leads me neatly on to the next section of this book.

HOLD UP!

Remember I asked you to make some notes on your planned strategy for growing your business at the beginning of this book?

Dig them out now and see if you want to reassess them.

You do?

Time for a new plan then.

Want help with it?

Go to: www.gycsf.co.uk/plan

and download your free marketing templates.

SUMMARY

Plan

Growing your business needs a plan. Now you are aware of how to grow your business get the plan written.

Time

Make time for your marketing. 20% of your time should be devoted to growing your business.

Quality Products

The quality of your products is a minimum requirement of your business.

Quality Equipment

Quality products need quality equipment and quality ingredients to produce them.

Remember: JFDI

PART 4

Chapter 9

Coffee & Coffee Equipment

I'm obviously in the coffee machine and coffee supply business so in this section I'm going to look at coffee machines and their differences as well as the coffees you can use in them.

It's basically a guide to the different types and their advantages and disadvantages.

Tools of the Trade

All your coffee shop equipment must be reliable and perform well. For this you need quality machines that you can rely on to work day in, day out.

A carpenter relies on his woodworking tools.

A butcher relies on his knives.

A mechanic on his spanners.

A plumber relies on his plumbing tools.

Every trade relies on having the right tools for the right job. And if you're using a tradesman to do a job for you, then you'd expect him to be using the correct tools for that job.

You are in the coffee shop trade and are no different. If your coffee machine isn't working, then you haven't got a coffee shop. Not only is it frustrating to have poor equipment but it's also time consuming and inefficient.

The main demand these days is for espresso machines and their related items. Other methods are still used, for example, cafetieres and filter machines. I'll cover these later but let's start, and concentrate on the espresso machine.

Espresso Coffee Systems

What does an Espresso Machine do?

Essentially they all force water through finely ground coffee at a pressure of 9 bar and a temperature of about 92 °C to produce an Espresso coffee.

In fact, it's all about the pressure!

If you don't know what 9 bar of pressure looks like, it's about 5 times the pressure of a car tyre or the pressure you would feel if you were 90 metres under water! There's a lot of pressure involved in making an espresso coffee, although not a large volume of water.

What are the differences in the machines?

There are three basic classes of machine:

Manual

Semi-automatic

Automatic

Manual

As the name suggests, you manually generate the pressure to produce the Espresso. These are the machines with the big handles on the front. The pressure is generated by pulling the handle down. This lifts a piston, compressing a large spring above it. As the piston reaches the top of the chamber, a small port allows water from the boiler to enter between the piston and a shower plate. When the handle is released the spring then pushes the piston down, seals off the water port, and forces the water though the shower plate and through the finely ground coffee to produce the Espresso. This type of machine has a set pressure derived from the spring and a set volume of water.

Advantages –

Useful for coffee carts and other situations where electrical power is limited, the boilers can be heated by gas as well.

Some people just prefer them for the theatre and feel of the process.

Disadvantages –

Pressure is fixed by the strength of the spring.

Needs a fair amount of physical force to use.

Volume of the espresso is fixed

Semi-automatic

The pressure in these machines is derived from an electric pump system. There is a switch, usually just above the group head, which turns the pump on and opens an inlet valve to force the water through the coffee. Here the volume of water is manually controlled by the operator. The water pressure is adjustable on the pump and can be set accurately using the built-in pressure gauge.

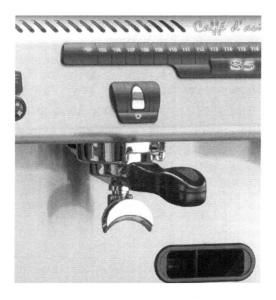

A Typical Semi-Automatic Coffee Machine with On/Off Button Operation

Advantages -

Cheaper than automatic machines.

Good for the Barista who likes total control

Disadvantages –

You need to know exactly what you're doing

Needs to be monitored all the time

Not suitable for most applications

Automatic

These are the most popular machines. Again, the pressure is provided by a pump, but the volume of water forced through the coffee is measured by small flow meters and the pump switched off automatically.

There are usually 4 programmable buttons: -

Single Ristretto (60% of an espresso, 18 ml.)

Single Espresso (30 ml.)

Double Ristretto (36 ml.)

Double Espresso (60 ml.)

The Ristretto is rarely used in this country so it's common practice to program both the single buttons for a single espresso and both the double buttons for double espressos.

There is also a free flow button which acts like the on/off switch on the semi-automatic machines. This is used for cleaning.

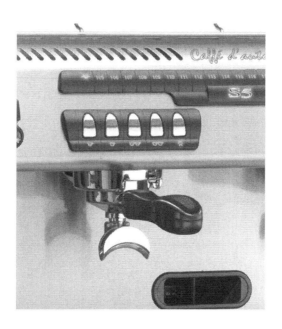

A Typical Automatic Coffee Machine with Programmed Button Pad

Advantages –

Easy to use

Looks after itself once the button is pressed

Disadvantages –

A bit more costly than Semi-Automatic Machines

Size of Machine

Machines come in a range of sizes: -

Compact - a 2 group machine with a small boiler

1 group

2 group

3 group

4 group

The group refers to the coffee making section on the machine, the picture overleaf is of a 2-group machine i.e. It can take two group handles (or portafilters).

A typical 2 group coffee machine

The compact and single group machines are more suited to bars and small restaurants. Their smaller boiler size makes them unsuitable for heavy use.

A standard 2 group machine is the basic requirement for busy restaurants or small coffee shops.

The 3 or 4 group machines are more suited for larger coffee shops and busy outlets and can be used with two grinders, one at each end.

If you also need large volumes of boiling water it can be quite a drain on a coffee machine, particularly the smaller machines. In this case I would always recommend that you use a separate water boiler for teas, etc.

Another option to consider in a busy environment is having two 2 group machines instead of one large machine (something to do with eggs and baskets!).

Other Variations

Steam / Water Valves

Twiddly knobs or flip lever? Somewhat of a personal choice but as one needs full power steam for foaming milk the flip lever is more efficient and easier to use.

Electronic or Pressure Switch Heat Control

Not obvious from the outside but cheaper machines tend to use the traditional pressure switch to turn the boiler elements on and off. Here the steam pressure is used to act on a set of bellows, which in turn, active a large set of electrical contacts. You can hear them clank in and out on these machines. The temperature swing is quite large compared to the more modern, solid state electronic control. Electronic control also does away with the mechanical contacts, which tend to burn out eventually.

Standard or Take-Away Machines

Take-away machines are simply machines that have a larger gap between the group handle and the drip tray allowing take-away cups to be used easily. There is usually a small shelf which can be lowered when normal cups are required.

If take-away is not the main use for your coffee machine, then it's just as easy to make the espresso in a small jug or container and transfer it to the larger take-away cup.

Integrated grinder

There are a few machines on the market that feature an integrated grinder built in to the traditional coffee machine. As coffee beans and ground coffee don't like heat or moisture, it is best to avoid these types of machine - you've also got all your eggs in one basket if either fail!

Full Electronic Control

Top of the range machines now come with some impressive features. They log every coffee made, the time taken to make it, advise on grinder settings and log information for engineers. Fault analysis with Wi-Fi connections is available and, as is the way of the world, these features will likely become more common place.

Auto-Milk Foaming

These devices automatically foam your milk to the correct temperature and consistency. Sounds like a great idea and can be useful when you first get a machine but, in my experience, everyone gives up using them as they get more confident with the process.

Types of Coffee

Machines can be set up for use with ready ground coffee, pods or capsules.

See:- Espresso Coffees for more details.

Espresso Grinders

If you're using coffee beans then choosing a good grinder is essential. The grinder is as important, if not more so, than the coffee machine. If your coffee beans aren't ground properly to start with, you can't expect the resulting coffee to be any good.

When adjusting a grinder, we're talking about fractions of a millimetre in particle size. The smallest of changes will affect the extraction time of your espresso shot. You'll also find that different coffee blends will usually require different grinder settings to get that perfect extraction time.

When choosing a grinder bear in mind that once the coffee beans are ground to a fine consistency, as required for an espresso, the coffee will oxidize rapidly and go stale. In fact, it is only good for a couple of hours, really good for about half an hour!

What are the options?

There are 2 main categories of grinder:

Grind and Dispense

Grind on Demand

Typical Grind & Dispense Grinder

Grind and dispense - the beans are ground into a dispensing or dosing chamber at the front of the grinder, and then measured doses of coffee can be dispensed as required.

Typical Grind on Demand Grinder

Grind on demand - here the coffee is ground as required. A timed dispense of coffee is deposited straight into the group handle basket.

Grind & Dispense

There are 3 operating types: -

Manual

Timer

Automatic

Manual

Grinds the coffee into the hopper just by switching on and off.

Advantages –

Cheapest

Disadvantages –

You need to monitor the levels. Easy to forget and leave the grinder running.

Timed

Uses a timer switch so the amount required can be judged, the further the timer switch is rotated the more coffee is ground.

Advantages –

Easy to keep levels of coffee right for busy and quiet periods.

Disadvantages –

You need to monitor the levels.

Automatic

Keeps the dispensing hopper permanently full.

Advantages –

Looks after itself

Disadvantages –

If the coffee isn't being used it will be going stale, particularly overnight.

If the grind needs altering, you have a whole hopper full of incorrectly ground coffee.

Other factors

Grind speed - A slow speed grinder is better than a fast speed one – it's important not to overheat the coffee before it is used, so a slow speed, high powered grinder is better than a high speed one. Speeds vary from about

800 rpm up to 1500 rpm, the later tend to be cheaper. A well-built lower speed grinder should last you years. And, even a 'slow' speed grinder can still grind the coffee faster than you can use it!

Grinder Blades - the standard types are flat. Coffee beans are fed into a hole in the middle of the stationary disc and are ground by the rotating bottom disc until the coffee is forced out of the gap at the sides. The stationary disc can be adjusted up and down to determine how fine the coffee is ground. It's the same principal as the mill stones of old.

Some grinders are fitted with conical blades, not so common and associated with the more expensive, slow speed grinders at the top of the range.

Built in Tamper - Many grinders feature a tamper system as well. There's more on tamping in the next couple of pages but it is very important to tamp the coffee in the group handle before inserting it into the coffee machine. A telescopic tamper (as shown on page 142) is the best. It is almost impossible to get the required tamping force with a fixed tamper where you're trying to lift the group handle up against it.

Grind On Demand

All 'grind on demand' grinders dispense a timed dose of coffee on demand. The majority use the flat style grinder blades and are usually fairly high speed - not so critical in this case as only a single or double dose of the coffee is being ground at any one time and it's going to be used straight away.

Advantages –

Provides the freshest dose of coffee every time.

Disadvantages –

Despite the higher grind speed, they are slower dispensing than a traditional grinder.

More expensive.

Adjusting can be tricky. Varying the grind will also vary the quantity of coffee ground in a given time, so timing will need to be adjusted as well.

Tamping

The reason for tamping the coffee is to produce an even, level bed of coffee and to eliminate pockets of air. The idea is to make sure all the water is forced through all the coffee to get a full extraction. It's recommended that up to 18 kg of force is used when tamping, Grind on demand grinders don't feature a tamper. Some other form of tamping is required.

The different tamping methods are:

Integral with a grinder

Many grind and dispense grinders have an integral tamper as I mentioned earlier. While this can suffice, a far better way of tamping is to use one of the following methods:

Hand Tamper

As the name suggests a simple device usually of a heavy metal base and wooden or plastic handle. The group handle is rested on a rubber mat and the coffee tamped manually by hand. Tampers come in a whole range of designs and can be quite a personal possession to a Barista.

Advantages –

Cheap, though fancy expensive models are available.

Disadvantages –

Pressure relies on the Barista.

Levelling relies on the Barista.

A busy Barista can develop a repetitive strain injury known as 'Barista's Wrist'

Click Tamper

This device is a variation on the hand tamper. As pressure is applied to the coffee the tamper clicks or 'breaks' once the correct pressure has been applied. This ensures that you're getting a consistent tamping pressure, as long as you use enough force to make the click happen!

Advantages –

The pressure applied is consistent.

Disadvantages –

More expensive

Levelling is Barista dependant.

Busy Baristas can develop 'Barista's Wrist'

Automatic

Here the operation is all automatic. The group handle is inserted in the device which automatically tamps the coffee level and to an adjustable, pre-set pressure. This takes all the guess work out of tamping ensuring a consistent, quality tamp.

Advantages –

The pressure can be adjusted and pre-set.

The pressure applied is consistent.

Levelling of the coffee is accurate and consistent.

Alleviates 'Barista's Wrist'

Disadvantages –

Most expensive.

.

Accessories

You've decided on a machine and a grinder. Now there are several accessories that are required to complete the kit.

These will often come bundled with a machine / grinder package but it's as well to be aware of the options, what you need and a couple of items you don't really need.

Calcium Treatment Unit

(or Water Filter)

The chances are that you are in a hard water area so you will require a calcium treatment unit. This will prevent scale from building up inside the coffee machine and will require an exchange unit fitting at regular intervals. This is an extra cost but is nothing compared to having a heavily scaled machine descaled. This would probably involve fitting new elements and other parts as well.

Secondary filter

Whether or not you are in a hard water area it is a good idea to fit a secondary micro mesh filter just before the water enters the coffee machine. The high pressure pumps in espresso machines have very fine tolerances and even small particles that enter can jam the mechanism.

Knockout Box

This is used to knock the spent coffee grounds from the group handle after the espresso is made. In a busy environment it can take quite a hammering and, due to space restrictions, is often placed under the grinder so it needs to be of robust construction. A box is not needed if you're using pods instead of a grinder, although a small one would be handy.

Foaming Jugs

A couple of different sized jugs is a good idea. Generally straight sided with a good pouring spout is best. Avoid the ones that are tapered (like an upside-down cone) it's difficult to foam the milk properly in these.

There are various models available, some light weight, some heavy, some coated with Teflon. At the end of the day it tends to be more of a personal choice.

Cups

Bowl shaped cups are the most popular and preferred by Baristas. They allow the coffee and milk to flow well and make the drink look appetising. This is particularly important if you want to produce latte art with the milk. The colour can have an effect as well, darker colours give the perception of a stronger drink, pink or flowery colours being perceived as sweeter. Sticking to white is usually the best thing.

Thermometer and Spatula

Not really needed if the milk is being foamed correctly. Most thermometers, unless you pay a lot of money for them, lag behind and don't give a true reading anyway. They also tend to get covered in splattered milk and end up all messy.

Again, a spatula is not necessary. If you are foaming the milk correctly, then it's quicker and easier to make the drinks without one.

Cloth

It may seem strange to mention a cloth here, but keeping your steam wand clean is vital. Always make sure you have a stock of clean cloths, for this purpose and this purpose alone.

Other Coffee Brewing Methods

Staying on the espresso theme, there are a couple of other ways of producing espresso based drinks.

Bean to Cup Machine

Best avoided. They are basically one machine trying to do too much and not really applicable to a coffee shop where quality is the focus. If you want to go down this route all I can say is - you've almost finished reading the wrong book. There are one or two good machines about but be prepared to spend a lot of money on one and you <u>will</u> need an expensive maintenance contract. On top of that, in my experience, they still breakdown.

Advantages –

Push button operation (when working).

Little staff training.

Disadvantages –

Expensive (for a half reliable machine)

Expensive maintenance.

Will breakdown.

Pod Systems

There are some dedicated commercial espresso pod systems around now and they do make very good espresso coffees. They can also sit next to traditional espresso kit and be used for producing speciality espressos. Some systems are modular, allowing you to build up a system as you go, some are manual water fill as well allowing them to be moved easily.

A commercial modular Espresso Pod System

Advantages –

Perfect espresso every time.

The coffee is always fresh

Little staff training.

Range of different espresso coffees.

Modular systems available.

Cheaper than traditional machines.

Ideal for small venues or behind bars.

Cheaper on electricity

Quick start up times

Easy to clean

No waste

Disadvantages –

Lack the theatre of a traditional machine.

Lower steam and water capacity.

Coffee more expensive

Capsule Machines

These machines are similar to pod systems, just designed to work with capsules instead. The only major difference is they involve more packaging and are therefore less environmentally friendly.

Filter Coffee Machines

Pour & Serve machines

These are the normal filter coffee machines with a couple of jugs that sit on hotplates. They use a filter grind coffee and typically brew 3 pints of coffee in about 5 minutes. They are normally manual fill and just plug into a 13amp socket. A useful backup to a traditional espresso machine setup. There are still a lot of people who like a good filter coffee, and at the time of writing filter coffee is forecast to be making a bit of a comeback. Coffee is usually brewed into glass jugs, kept hot on a hot plate. An alternative is to use a flask system where the brewed coffee is stored in a stainless-steel vacuum flask.

Advantages –

Usually manual water fill

Useful for functions for black coffee

Good back up to an espresso system

Disadvantages –

Coffee brewed into glass jugs can stew if not used reasonable quickly

Bulk Brew Coffee machines

For larger or busy venues, a bulk brew coffee machine is often the answer. The latest models allow you to brew varying quantities, and adjust parameters such as temperature, pre-soak volumes, pre-soak times and brew time. (Pre-soaking is where a small amount of water is added to the coffee before the main brew to pre-wet it and aid extraction). These settings can be changed and stored in order to get the best out of your filter coffee. It is often surprising to see how a small change in one or two of these parameters can affect the overall taste of the coffee. Different blends of coffee will require different machine settings to get the best from them. Once a blend of coffee is selected these parameters can be supplied on a memory stick to set the machine up for that particular blend.

Advantages –

Good for large volumes of coffee

Modern machines can be programmed to get the best from the coffee

Plumbed in

Disadvantages –

Usually require high powered electrical supplies

Cafetiere

Not used so much these days but still popular with some venues.

Advantages –

Minimum amount of equipment required

Made freshly for individual orders

Disadvantages –

Can be sludgy in the cup

Messy coffee grounds to dispose of

Equipment Suppliers

Always buy from a reputable supplier who knows what they are talking about. Some catering equipment companies sell coffee machines and grinders, but in my experience, they know nothing about the features you should be looking for.

On more than one occasion I've been to a site where the equipment has been supplied and installed by such a company. It's usually cheap, not always suitable for the job in hand and invariably the installers have no idea how to set up or program the machine and grinder.

It's not just catering equipment companies that can supply unsuitable equipment though, as the following anecdote shows.

I was helping a customer set up some equipment ready for a staff training session in a new venue. They buy their coffee from me but unfortunately the venue had organised and bought the equipment separately from a coffee machine supplier. There was a flashy looking 'grind on demand' grinder along with a 3group machine. We tried for over an hour to obtain a consistent grind and dose weight. After wasting over a kilo of coffee the espresso extraction times were still all over the place. We gave up and called the supplier. He stated that the 'grinder was not good enough for a busy outlet and wouldn't use it with that size of coffee machine'. What? If he knows it's a pile of shit, why on earth is he selling it? It wasn't good enough for any sort of job. Well, a door stop, perhaps.

In my experience Italian made espresso equipment is usually the best, probably because they were the original country to develop the method and create an espresso culture.

A reputable supplier should: -

- Recommend the correct equipment

- Install and program the equipment

- Train staff on:

    Use of the equipment

    All safety aspects

    How to make the various drinks

    Cleaning procedures

- Provide a full back-up service

SUMMARY

Equipment

Make sure you have the right equipment for your outlet.

Advice

There is a vast array of options on equipment, get advice on what you need and the services required for it.

Quality

Quality equipment is an investment.

Suppliers

Buy from a reputable supplier.

Remember: Your coffee machines are the tools of your trade, don't skimp on quality

Chapter 8

Coffee

A bar manager once said to me that 'coffee is coffee'. That's a bit like saying 'wine is wine' or 'beer is beer'. There's a vast range of coffees and coffee blends to choose from.

As with grapes there are many varieties of coffee bush and they're grown in a range of soils, climatic conditions, and at varying altitudes, all of which will have an effect on the flavour of the resulting coffee beans.

There are many good books on coffee and coffee varieties, so I won't delve into it here in any detail, I'll just cover the basics.

Coffee Varieties

Coffee bushes are grown in equatorial regions. There are two main classes of coffee bean, Robusta and Arabica.

Robusta coffee is grown at low altitudes and tends to have a strong earthy taste with a lot of body. The beans also have a higher caffeine content than the Arabica's. Robusta's are largely used in instant coffees but have a role to play in espresso blends and filter coffees.

Arabica coffees are grown at higher altitudes and tend to have more delicate, interesting flavour notes. These can be floral, citrusy, chocolaty, etc.

In both of those statements I used the word 'tend' because, like most things, it isn't all cut and dried. There are some Arabicas with plenty of body and there are some Robustas that can stand alone as far as flavour and taste goes.

Overall there are a vast range of different flavour and strength variations.

Coffee Processing

Coffee is, of course, a natural product and as such the same beans from the same farm can vary from season to season. After harvesting and drying the green beans are then graded. A reputable roaster will sample the crops before placing an order and then check the main delivery against the original standard sample. As coffee batches can vary, blends are often adjusted to maintain the quality and flavour profile of that particular blend. A lot of people are paid a lot of money to taste, grade and blend these coffees.

Blended coffees are often thought to be the poor relation of Single Estate coffees. But a well-blended coffee can harness the various qualities of the constituent beans and produce an excellent, well balanced, pleasant drink.

Most espresso coffees are blends, particularly true of Italian Style espressos.

Another variable is roasting, coffees can be roasted to a greater or lesser extent, lightly roasted beans tend to give an acidic sweeter coffee where-as dark roasted will impart more of the roasting flavours and there's a range of roast profiles between these extremes. Cheaper beans are usually over roasted, this brings out a burnt flavour which compensates for the lack of flavour in the beans. Interestingly Northern Italian coffees tend to be lightly roasted whereas Southern Italian coffees are dark roasted. This is historical because the North used to be relatively affluent and could afford the better quality coffees, the South was poorer and the cheaper coffee was over roasted to compensate for its lack of flavour. Traditions die hard!

Cheap coffees also tend to be harsh and have 2 undesirable side effects.

1. They tend to leave an unpleasant aftertaste.

2. Often lead to a dry rough feeling in the back of the throat.

There are a vast range of coffees at a range of prices. The cheaper ones should be avoided and some at the very pricey end are over hyped.

At the end of the day your customer wants a pleasant drink that will make them want to return or even have a second coffee there and then.

Coffees for Espresso

There are 4 options here:

Coffee Beans
Pre-ground Coffee
Coffee Pods
Coffee Capsules

Coffee Beans

This is the most common form for making espresso coffees used with a grinder to produce the fine grind required.

Advantages –

Most cost effective

Grinder can be adjusted to get the best from the coffee

Disadvantages

Requires a grinder

Pre-ground Coffee

Available in bulk packs or sachets

Advantages –

No grinder required.

Useful in pre-portioned sachets for decaf where a separate grinder is not justified.

Disadvantages –

Grind is not adjustable to suit the machine or conditions.

Bulk packs will go stale once opened.

Coffee Pods & Capsules

Pods are a bit like tea bags, except they're filled with hard packed espresso coffee. Capsules are like pods but the coffee is packed in a plastic or aluminium capsule.

Advantages –

No grinder required.

Individually packed for freshness.

Good for the smaller outlet or offices.

Cleaner than loose ground beans.

Simple to use.

Extraction good as the water has no option other than to pass through the pod or capsule.

Produce an excellent espresso in dedicated machines. (See: - Other Systems)

Clean.

Disadvantages –

More expensive.

Pods are usually a bit of a compromise in a traditional machine.

Coffees for Filter and Cafetiere

These are often supplied as country specific blends, Colombian, Kenya and so on, though blends are also available. To preserve freshness and consistency when brewed these coffees are usually portion packed to suit the equipment being use.

Filter coffees are usually a medium grind, while cafetiere coffee needs to be a course grind. You will often find retail packs packed as an omni-grind, basically a compromise to make the pack of coffee suitable for both filter and cafetiere.

Artisan Coffee Roasters

Artisan coffee roasters seem to be popping up everywhere these days, a good thing in a way because it's driving the awareness of coffee in the right direction.

Many are providing a good quality product, but, they're not always what they seem.

I know of one company that gives the impression they roast their own coffee when they don't and at least two others that, although they do roast coffee in their small roaster, use a commercial roaster to provide the volume of product they need. I even know of yet another one that, despite advertising where their coffee is roasted, has some of it roasted in a different country altogether.

 I supplied some coffee equipment to a customer who wanted to use an Artisan roaster for their supplies. I got a call sometime later to say the grinder wasn't working. On inspection, it turned out that the coffee was stale. You cannot adjust a grinder fine enough to get a good extraction using stale coffee. In their continued attempts to adjust it they'd managed to overheat the grinder and, luckily, the £5 capacitor had failed instead of the grinder motor burning out. I contacted said roaster and explained that he'd supplied stale coffee, to which he replied 'What are you talking about, coffee doesn't go stale.' Excuse me!

Quality of Coffee

As I said earlier coffees are like wine, there are hundreds of different options and qualities of coffee beans, and like anything else top quality coffee beans attract the top prices.

I was talking to a chap who worked in London, tasting batches of coffee beans that were to be sold or auctioned, most of it was good quality, but he told me there was always some real rubbish that shouldn't have even been for sale, but he says, he was always amazed that someone always bought it. Wouldn't tell me who though!

The quality of coffee bean is important but just as your coffee shop needs quality equipment so does the roaster. Modern commercial roasters have some impressive equipment, from high tech sampling machines to ensure consistency of the green beans, to colour spectrographs for checking roast colours and, of course, computer controlled roasters designed to provide the perfect roast.

Packaging is an important factor as well. Roasted coffee beans do not get on well with heat, moisture, sunlight and above all, oxygen. Coffee oxidizes and goes stale rapidly. A further complication here is that freshly roasted beans will 'gas off' for a period after roasting. Therefore, packaging should be sealed but have some form of one way valve set in the bag to let this gas escape.

Pre-ground filter coffees are allowed to gas off for a short period before packing. When packed, the coffee sachet or bag is flushed with Nitrogen to eliminate oxygen from it.

The Best Coffee

I'm often asked "Which is the best coffee?" Jamaican Blue Mountain? 100% Arabica? Single Origin? Fairtrade? And so on.

The answer is the one you like, more importantly though, it's the one your customers like.

Certified coffees

A note on certified coffees. You can now get Fairtrade, Rain Forest Alliance, Bird Friendly, Gorilla Friendly, Shade Grown, etc. etc. It's almost like pick a charity - should you want to support one.

Coffee Suppliers

Again, as with the equipment, pick a reputable coffee supplier who knows about coffee.

I set up a restaurant with some coffee equipment a few years ago, but the owner subsequently decided to buy his coffee from his friend, a wine merchant. The wine merchant apparently saw a way of increasing his sales by selling coffee beans alongside his wine. He had no idea about how to adjust the machine to suit his coffee beans. Different coffee beans will often need a different grinder setting and sometimes a different temperature setting on the coffee machine to get the best from them.

A reputable supplier should: -

- Recommend appropriate coffees

- Provide information on the blend of coffee

- Adjust equipment to get the best extraction

- Train staff on:

  How to get the best from the coffee

  For espresso coffees:

  Barista Skills

  How to make the coffee drinks

- Provide back-up advice when needed.

SUMMARY

Coffee

Make sure you have the right coffee for your equipment.

Advice

There is a vast array of options on coffees, get advice on what will suit you and your customers.

Quality Products

Providing quality coffee drinks is a minimum requirement for your business.

Suppliers

Buy from a reputable supplier.

Remember: Your customers are the ones who have to like your coffee

Chapter 9

Costs

I've added this chapter as a basic guide to the costs involved with coffee machines. The figures quoted are based on costs at the time of writing and will obviously change over time. I say change but undoubtedly they'll go up!

The costs may vary but the % figures quoted should remain about the same.

Coffee

Coffee is traded in US dollars and is also a commodity, bought and sold on the futures market which not only makes coffee prices dependent on crop yields and world demand but on exchange rates and commodity forecasts as well. A mine field!

Coffee is, however, one of the highest gross margin products you will be dealing with.

The cost of an espresso shot is about 8p at rock bottom, about 12p for a good quality coffee and going up from there. So, the difference between a rock bottom price and a good quality bean is about 4p a shot or if you sell 3% more coffee to your existing customers because it's good quality, and they like the experience, you are better off. There is no excuse for not selling quality coffee at these kinds of prices. In fact, it's to your advantage to do so.

Equipment

There's several ways to pay for your equipment.

Buying outright, leasing or renting.

Buying Out Right

Overleaf is a table showing the estimated payback times for espresso equipment. Please note that the table doesn't consider the costs of staff, power or other overheads. It does, however, illustrate the profits that can be made from your coffee sales and how quickly the costs of the equipment can be covered.

For example:

Your equipment cost is £ 4500

You sell a cappuccino for £ 2.75

On average, you sell 125 per day

Your ingredient cost is, say, 20p per drink.

Then the profit from your coffee will cover the cost of the equipment in 17 days (in bold).

Note that the profit from a further couple of days trading would cover the extra for a far better set up.

As this illustrates it is not worth skimping on the quality of your coffee equipment.

Machine payback time

Coffee Sale Price   =   £2.75

Coffee Cost Price   =   £0.20

Profit less VAT   =   £2.12

Drinks sold per day

Cost	50	75	100	**125**	150	175	200
3000	29	19	15	12	10	9	8
3500	33	22	17	14	11	10	9
4000	38	25	19	15	13	11	10
4500	43	29	22	**17**	15	13	11
5000	48	32	24	19	16	14	12
5500	52	35	26	21	18	15	13
6000	57	38	29	23	19	17	15

Table of payback time, in days, for different machine costs and different no of drinks sold per day.

PLEASE NOTE: This table is for guidance only.

Leasing

Leasing is a form of rental, arranged through a dedicated leasing company. They charge a monthly rental based on a lease rate, for example, £38 per £1000 for a three-year lease, though the rate varies depending on the status of the applicant. Funding for leasing has been difficult over the past few years due to the financial crisis and the tight-fisted banks.

Anyone would think the catering industry was responsible for the banking crisis instead of their own failings!

Having said that, the situation is improving, gradually, and more leasing applications are being accepted.

If you are considering this method of funding your equipment there are additional fees you need to be aware of:

1   Set up fee.

2   Annual maintenance fee. (Though I can't see how they justify that one!)

3   Final payment, which must be made through a third party if you want to own the equipment at the end of the lease period. This is usually equivalent to another months' lease rental.

4   Insurance will often be required if you can't show that the equipment is covered by your own business policy.

Continuity System

Some companies will offer a continuity system. This involves renting directly from a coffee company with a package that includes maintenance, servicing and a basic level of coffee supplies. Additional supplies can be added as and when needed. New equipment is supplied every 3 years.

It's a convenient method of spreading the costs and making sure the equipment is always up to date and as reliable as it can be. This system also allows you to budget more accurately as monthly costs are pretty much fixed.

SUMMARY

Coffee

Buy quality coffee, it's a few pence per cup.

Buying Equipment

Payback times are short, don't skimp on the quality of your equipment.

Leasing Equipment

Leasing is a convenient way of spreading costs but be aware of additional fees.

Continuity System

Convenient for fixing costs and ensuring a continual service and coffee supply.

Remember: Invest in quality coffee and equipment

<u>Remember: -</u>

Take Action

Work On Your Business not In It

The Majority are Wrong

You are in the marketing business

Generating your Avatar is a vital step in your marketing strategy.

Become the Expert to your customers.

Sell Constantly

Keep things fresh

Profit is Sanity

Your coffee machines are the tools of your trade, don't skimp on quality

Your customers are the ones who have to like your coffee

Invest in quality coffee and equipment

And Finally: -

JFDI

For help on your marketing and planning go to:

www.gycsf.co.uk/plan